The Long Night

Readings and Stories to Help You through Depression

JESSICA KANTROWITZ

FORTRESS PRESS
MINNEAPOLIS

THE LONG NIGHT
Readings and Stories to Help You through Depression

Cover design: Olga Grlic

Print ISBN: 978-1-5064-5664-5

eBook ISBN: 978-1-5064-5665-2

In loving memory of Jason Heanssler and Rob Ghirardi

Contents

The Long Night: Invitation

> Let us go then, you and I,
> When the evening is spread out against the sky
> Like a patient etherized upon a table;
> Let us go, through certain half-deserted streets,
> The muttering retreats
> Of restless nights in one-night cheap hotels
> And sawdust restaurants with oyster-shells:
> Streets that follow like a tedious argument
> Of insidious intent
> To lead you to an overwhelming question . . .
> Oh, do not ask, "What is it?"
> Let us go and make our visit."
>
> ~T.S. Eliot, The Love Song of J. Alfred Prufrock[1]

Come for a walk with me, my friend. I know you are tired. I know that sorrow has settled into your bones like the ache from an old wound. Come with me anyway. Lean on my arm. It is only a few steps to the forest's entrance and a few more to a bench where we can rest. I know the colors have gone out of your life, and you cannot rouse yourself to remember them. I know. In the twilight, the world is muted, and it will not sting as much when you can only see grey. We can turn back anytime. Your bed will be waiting for you. Just come out for a few minutes.

Come for a walk with me, dear one. I know that walking is hard, and your muscles ache; you feel a weariness that does not pass no matter how much you sleep. I know that talking feels impossible, and you fear that if you do speak, you will be unable to stop and will wear me out with your words, crying over and over of your pain and despair. It's all right, my friend. You do not have to speak, and if you do, there is space in my heart and in the forest for all your pain. There is space for you, my friend, believe me. Come and weep or come and be silent. Just come.

Come for a walk with me, Beloved. I know you feel nothing but loneliness and being with people makes you feel even more alone. I know you feel lost and left behind, abandoned by friends and by the God you once adored. I know you feel a betrayal so sharp and real that sometimes you cannot breathe. I know that when I call you God's Beloved it rings hollow, that if I speak the words of poetry or scripture that used to mean something to you, they now taste like sand in your mouth. Come into the whispering darkness of the trees at twilight and listen to the scripture they speak. Come into the shadows of the oaks and lindens until the darkness outside matches the darkness in your soul. Then listen to how the dark speaks its own language, one you could not hear in the bright light of day. If you do not hear it tonight, that's okay, too. I will walk you home, regardless. I will trust your soul, regardless. Beloved, I will.

Come for a walk with me, sister, brother, sibling. I have been here before and can maybe be a sister to you. Let me hold your hand as you learn to walk in this new world. You have been walking for years in the daylight, but this—this westering world where the shadows trip you as surely as the stones—is new territory. It is hard to move here, I know, but you can do it. We can do it together. Underneath your despair I can see that spark of strength. Not everyone will realize how much it took for you to step outside for these few minutes, but I know. Even if you collapse back in bed for the next twenty-three and a half hours, I know that the courage and strength it takes to face the world for those few moments are almost unimaginable. I know you feel so weak, little sibling, but you are strong in ways few people will ever know.

Come for a walk with me, dear reader. I know you have questions I cannot answer, and there are things in your life I cannot understand. But let's go out together tonight, away from the cacophony of the city, of the daylight, of the world wide web. Let's go into the dusky woods together, the quiet dappled evening where the trolls and other monsters cannot follow. Let's find one of the Ten Thousand Places, one of the hidden places where it's okay to be sad and unsure, where it's okay to ask our overwhelming questions and okay to let the answer be that we don't know. I know you're tired, and the day has already been far too long. You can rest soon, dear one, I promise. Only first, come, come for a walk.

Notes

1. T. S. Eliot, *Prufrock and Other Observations* (London: The Egoist, 1917), 9–16.

1. My Own Long Night

> This book . . . was written during the most diffi-
> cult period of my life. That was a time of extreme
> anguish, during which I wondered whether I
> would be able to hold on to my life. Everything
> came crashing down—my self-esteem, my
> energy to live and work, my sense of being
> loved, my hope for healing, my trust in God . . .
> everything. Here I was, a writer about the spiri-
> tual life, known as someone who loves God and
> gives hope to people, flat on the ground and
> in total darkness. What had happened? I had
> come face to face with my own nothingness. It
> was as if all that had given my life meaning was
> pulled away and I could see nothing in front of
> me but a bottomless abyss.
>
> ~Henri Nouwen[1]

I want you to know that I'm thinking of you as I write
this. I want you to know that this whole book is a prayer
for you, a prayer for my kindred souls who have fallen
into a seemingly endless pit with sheer sides, no handholds, and no discernible way to pull yourselves out. I
know that the words, "I'm praying for you," have lost
all meaning. Lots of people have been praying for
you—YOU have been praying for you—for so long that

the words have wilted and dulled. So, I want to tell you exactly what I mean when I say this book is a prayer for you.

By prayer I mean sitting next to you, waiting with you, for however long it takes. By prayer I mean that I believe you, that I know you are not lazy or rebellious or unfaithful. By prayer I mean that I believe that you are trying as hard as you can, maybe even too hard. I believe that you are doing the very best you can, regardless of how far you scramble forward or sink backward today. By prayer I mean that there are no deadlines; you don't just get grace until I get tired of you or until I determine that grace isn't working and it's time for tough love.

This book is a prayer for you, but by prayer I don't mean that I think God is angry at you and I am trying to change God's mind. I don't mean that God is somewhere else, and I am begging God to come here. God is already with you. God is already sitting next to you, waiting with you, for however long it takes. God knows that you are not lazy or rebellious or unfaithful. God knows that you are trying as hard as you can, maybe even too hard. God knows that you are doing the very best you can regardless of how far you scramble forward or sink backward today. God is not offering you short-term grace until God gets tired of you or until God decides that grace isn't working and it's time for tough love. God is there for the long haul. Grace is there for the long haul.

This book is a prayer for you, but by prayer I don't mean sympathy or pity, me looking down at you as I stand above it all. This book is an offer of empathy. We might not have everything in common, and you may be suffering in ways that I never did, but I offer up what I went through, my story and my pain. My prayer for you comes from that pain. I offer you, not answers, but my own suffering, my own struggles. And the reason I offer those is because that's what God offered me.

****

It was when I was thirty-four that everything fell apart. It was a "perfect storm" of stressors. I was having difficulty with relationships in the intentional religious community where I lived, my job was confusing and challenging, and the migraines that I'd had for most of my life had gotten worse. And then there was the depression. I think I'd probably been depressed off and on throughout my adolescence, but the first time I felt I'd walked straight off a cliff and into that pit was my senior year in college. It was horrific and terrifying, and I spent the next twelve years running from it.

Back then I thought I'd shaken depression off by graduating college, ending a bad relationship, and moving away from where the depression had found me. I played happy music, watched the gorgeous sunsets at the beach near where I'd moved, and vowed that I'd never fall into that pit again. For the next twelve years, whenever I felt the depression coming, I'd run. Moving and breaking up with a boy had helped once, so whenever I felt that particular sadness, that hollow feeling in my stomach and ache in my chest and arms, I tried to find something to change. If I wasn't in a relationship, I looked for some equivalent life change. I moved a lot. I took time off of grad school then reen-rolled; I quit my job and found a new one; I lived by myself, then with friends, and finally I moved back in with my parents. I moved from the North Shore of Massachusetts to Maine, then to Boston and back to Maine, and back to Boston again for my final internship for my master's degree. When I was thirty-two, I moved into the intentional religious community in Boston where I would stay for the next seven years.

At the same time that I moved into the community, I also started a job with a Christian parachurch orga-nization that did campus ministry. I had never fit a job description more perfectly. My Master of Divinity degree, my experience working with international stu-dents both in Boston and overseas, and my other min-istry experiences all lined up. It felt like I was finally headed somewhere in life, like God's plan for me was coming to fruition. For so long I'd worried that there was nothing I was good at, nothing I could do for a real career. I praised God for guiding me and redeem-ing the wandering. The community was great that first year, too. At thirty-two years old, I felt like I was finally beginning to find my path.

Around that time, I shared with my housemates that I was feeling a strange sadness in the evenings, just in the evenings. Then the sadness began to spread to the mornings. I began having insomnia, and my migraines worsened. Things began to be difficult at work and in the community. Almost worse than any of that, though, was that the spiritual practices I'd done for years didn't provide the same sense of peace and con-nection with God that they had so many times before.

I wrote an email to my friend that winter that just said, "Sleep is broken. Prayer is broken. How did they break?"

Eventually there came a crisis point. A weekend when I was supposed to help lead a retreat coincided with the start of two new medications prescribed by my neurologist for the migraines. I took them on a Thursday afternoon, and by that evening, it became clear that I was having a bad reaction to the new meds: anxiety, racing thoughts, despair, and thoughts of suicide that seemed more real than ever before. I emailed my supervisors and told them that I wasn't able to make the retreat, then I took a sleeping pill. When I woke up, feeling completely out of it but better emotionally, I had several messages from work. They didn't fire me, but I was on probation and told that my behavior would have to change. I finally realized I couldn't go on like this anymore.

I quit my ministry job and spent the next several months mostly in bed. It was a bleak time, but I was surprised to find a kind of peace in giving up. I was finally listening to what my body and spirit had been trying to tell me for a long time: I needed to rest.

After a while, I switched neurologists and found medications that somewhat helped with the migraines, and I began taking an anti-anxiety med to help even out my mood. I took a nanny job and started a freelance editing business for graduate students. Things continued to be hard in the community, but I felt myself slowly regaining equilibrium. I started jogging even though I had to do it in the evenings so I could sleep off the invariable migraine it brought on. I found moments of joy and peace with the toddler I was caring for, especially on days when we could get outside to Boston's many parks.

I practiced contemplative prayer along with biofeed-back and cognitive behavioral therapy. I saw various counselors though it was hard to find one that was the right fit. And after eight years, I moved out of the community that had been such a source of joy, pain, family, and conflict, and I found even more healing in the solitude of an apartment shared with a good friend.

My journey has been long. As I write this, almost ten years have passed since the worst of the depression and migraines. The migraines are still a daily struggle, but I have learned what I need to do to take care of myself, and I'm able to work enough to pay the bills. The depression returns occasionally, but I know what I need to do to get through it, and I know what I would need to do if it ever came for a longer stay.

That is the story of my own long night. Yours will be different, and your ways of healing will be different. I cannot say how long it will take for you, how long the long night will be. I'm not here to tell you what you need to do to heal, though I can tell you what helped me. All I want to do is to tell you a little of my own story so that hopefully you will feel that you are not alone in yours.

And that is also what I mean by prayer: That you are not alone.

****

Phew, okay, are you still with me? It can be hard to concentrate when the depression is bad. Feel free to take breaks, sleep for a while, cry if you need to. I'll be here when you get back.

Notes

1. Henri Nouwen, *The Inner Voice of Love* (New York: Image, 1998), xiii.

2. Companions on the Road

Two are better than one,
because they have a good return for their labor:
If either of them falls down,
one can help the other up.
But pity anyone who falls
and has no one to help them up.
Also, if two lie down together,
they will keep warm.
But how can one keep warm alone?
Though one may be overpowered,
two can defend themselves.
A cord of three strands is not quickly broken.[1]

For me, the long night of that major depressive episode lasted more than two years. Many of my friends and family could not fully understand what I was going through, and I felt very alone. But I had a good friend, Matteo, who also struggled with depression and other health issues. He came alongside me and offered me passages from writers who had been through similar struggles. I clung to pieces of hope from authors he introduced me to and from others I was already familiar with but whose words took on a deeper meaning with the depression, authors like Henri Nouwen, Madeleine L'Engle, George MacDonald,

Jeanne Guyon, Gerard Manley Hopkins, St. Teresa of Avilla, John of the Cross, and Thomas Merton. Their words were lifelines for me.

We need companions to travel alongside us, and we need those who have gone ahead of us who can say, "Yes, I understand exactly how hard this is. I have been through it, myself. And I made it through." In this book, I will introduce you to some writers who have been those companions for me in the hope that they can be for you as well. And maybe I can add myself to their number. The writer of Ecclesiastes asks, "Who can keep warm alone?"[2] But we are not alone. As another biblical writer says, "We are surrounded by a great cloud of witnesses."[3]

Henri Nouwen's story and his writing were particularly meaningful to me. He was a Catholic priest, professor, and writer whose work on the spiritual life touched many. He wrote about God's love in a profound and intimate way, and he referred to himself and others as God's Beloved, capitalized, since that is our identity and therefore our name. He was known and respected internationally, and he preached and taught all over the world, but it was not until age fifty-three, when he moved into L'Arche, a community that cared for people with intellectual and developmental disabilities, that he felt he had found his true home.

It was during that time at L'Arche, however, that he experienced a period of devastation and grief so overwhelming that he had to take several months off to address it. "Everything came crashing down," he wrote, "my self-esteem, my energy to live and work, my sense of being loved, my hope for healing, my trust in God."[4]

Nouwen went into intensive counseling with two people who gave him, "psychological and spiritual attention . . . and kept gently moving me from one day to the next, holding on to me as parents hold a wounded child."[5]

After each counseling session Nouwen wrote to himself in a journal to record his insights and discoveries. This journal was intended to be private, but, nearly ten years later, his friends convinced him that others could benefit from these insights and so the book, *The Inner Voice of Love* was published. It was this book that my friend Matteo gave me when my own life came crashing down.

In that slim volume, I found so many parallels to my experience. Nouwen was living in community when he wrote, and much of what he wrote resonated with my own experiences in my religious community. He wrote of finding that welcoming community and feeling loved and accepted only to experience his lowest time shortly after. He writes that it was "precisely at that time I fell apart—as if I needed a safe place to hit bottom!" That felt true of my experience in community as well.

Though he was a priest and an author, Nouwen's writing, particularly in *The Inner Voice of Love*, is so raw that it speaks to the basic human experience of searching for community. When I found myself struggling to find my place in my community and to succeed at my ministry job, Nouwen's words to himself spoke deeply to me:

> You have not yet fully found your place in your community. Your way of being present to your community may require times of absence, prayer, writing, or solitude. ... Your community needs you, but maybe not as a constant presence . . . your community also needs your creative absence.[6]

This offered me a glimpse of what I truly needed—to step back from leadership, rest, and examine my true calling. Even though it would be a while before I was able to act on that advice, his words stuck with me and comforted me.

I noted another parallel between Nouwen and I. He had formed a close friendship at L'Arche that was "interrupted" when his needs became too much for his friend: He writes, "this deeply satisfying friendship became the road to my anguish, because soon I discovered that the enormous space that had been opened for me could not be filled by the one who had opened it."[7] I experienced something similar with my friend Matteo as my depression deepened, and I began to rely too much on his support. My other friendships, too, were strained as I began to need more from my friends than I had before.

Above all, Nouwen helped me to understand that there was a way through the incredible pain I was experiencing. With his help, I learned how and when to delve into that pain. His words help me see that, "Yes, you must go to the place of your pain, but only when you have gained some new ground."[8] I learned to trust that even when the pain of depression and migraines stretched out over months and years, it would not last forever. Nouwen says, "You have to begin to trust that your feeling of emptiness is not the final experience, that beyond it is a place where you are being held in love."[9]

Nouwen made it through that time though there were days he felt sure he wouldn't survive. I made it through my own worst time of depression. And when I sat down to write this book, I realized that what I would most like to offer people is a book to hold in their hand the way I held Nouwen's *The Inner Voice of Love*. I want to offer you my own experience—the same way Nouwen offered his—as a source encouragement and evidence that we can make it through. Nouwen wrote in the second person because he was writing to himself, but that "you" resonates because we all experience pain. *You will survive*, I tell myself, and I have, and so I turn to my neighbor, to my readers, and say: You will survive, too. I was not alone, and therefore I know that you are not alone either.

You've made it through another breath, another day. And now you've made it through another chapter! Rest. Breathe. Henri and I will be here when you come back. And I have other friends to introduce you to, other companions along the road.

Notes

1. Eccl 4:9–12.
2. Eccl 4:11.
3. Heb 12:1.
4. Nouwen, *The Inner Voice*, xiii.
5. Nouwen, *The Inner Voice*, xvi.
6. Nouwen, *The Inner Voice*, 68.
7. Nouwen, *The Inner Voice*, xv.
8. Nouwen, *The Inner Voice*, 26.
9. Nouwen, *The Inner Voice*, 26. Chapter 3: God Suffers with Us

3. God Suffers with Us

Suffering invites us to place our hurts in larger hands. In Christ we see God suffering—for us. And calling us to share in God's suffering love for a hurting world. The small and even overpowering pains of our lives are intimately connected with the greater pains of Christ. Our daily sorrows are anchored in a greater sorrow and therefore a larger hope. Absolutely nothing in our lives lies outside the realm of God's judgment and mercy.[1]

~Henri Nouwen

I'm writing this now with the perspective and hindsight of nearly a decade. I try to remember what it felt like to be in the pit—in the depths of a depression—a time when I didn't know how to get through or even if it would ever end. But our minds are programmed to forget the full intensity of extreme pain. And I've worked hard to release it from my body through centering prayer, biofeedback, yoga, therapy, exercise, and countless deep, slow breaths. (I'll tell you more about all those things in the coming chapters.)

When I began writing this book, I didn't want to climb back down into that pit, but I had to find a way to write from my own experience of being there. So I tied a rope around my waist and lowered myself carefully down into my old emails, journal entries, and blog posts. I interviewed my younger self. How did you feel? What was it like? And I remembered this:

My plans wrecked. My body wrecked as well—in constant pain and weakness. Lying in bed for months because my head hurt too much to move. Avoiding people because the pain in my spirit made it impossible to chat about ordinary things. Too tired to get out of bed, but too overwhelmed with anxious thoughts to actually rest. Thinking back to the person I used to be—clever, funny, and wise—and wondering if I would ever be those things again. Reaching out to a God who seemed to have stepped away just when I needed God the most.

It was during one of those dark days, in bed and in pain, that I ordered a little crucifix online. The churches I'd grown up in had embraced the symbolism of an empty cross, focusing instead on the resurrection more than Christ's sufferings. But I knew that meditating on Jesus as he suffered on the cross was an important practice to some Christians, and I was willing to try anything to gain some felt-connection to God. I had hoped to find some understanding, some clarity, in Hebrews 4:14–16, a passage that always seemed so hopeful:

> Therefore, since we have a great high priest who has ascended into heaven, Jesus the Son of God, let us hold firmly to the faith we profess. For we do not have a high priest who is unable to empathize with our weaknesses, but we have one who has been tempted in every way, just as

we are—yet he did not sin. Let us then approach God's throne of grace with confidence, so that we may receive mercy and find grace to help us in our time of need.[2]

What does it mean that Jesus is a high priest who can empathize with our weakness? Empathy implies that he has gone through it himself. Did Jesus have migraines? Was he afflicted with a chemical imbalance that caused his mind to sink into the pit of depression? Did he have days when he struggled to get out of bed for more than a half an hour at a time?

When the crucifix I ordered finally arrived, I took out the little plastic Jesus. It seemed so strange. It was just a little Jesus doll when what I wanted was the real man, as present in my heart, mind, and spirit as he used to feel. But one day, when the pain was at its worst, I placed my fingers on the nails in Jesus's hands, studied his face and his body, and began to cry. I understood: Jesus was in pain, too. He was suffering, too. I might not have understood why it was happening to me or why God wouldn't answer my prayers to take the pain away, but at that moment I knew that Jesus was in it with me. Somehow whether he'd known the specific pain of migraines and depression on earth didn't matter; I knew that he understood. For the days and months to come I laid in bed, clutching the crucifix and crying.

I'd wanted God to heal me, but instead God had offered me empathy in my pain. All my life, I'd wanted to be like Jesus in his witty repartee, his compassion, and his ability to comfort and heal. But instead, I found I related most to his twisted form on the cross, eyes shut in pain, not yet dead, not yet resurrected, not yet ascended.

On my little crucifix, Jesus's features were not twisted in agony. If you didn't know better you might almost think he looked peaceful. But I thought that I recognized the movement inward that a long-suffering spirit makes. It is close to meditation. You have less to do with the world, with what is going on around you. Physical and emotional sensations take over, and then somehow, you sink below those sensations to a deeper place. I have experienced this kind of sinking and focus when the migraines are at their worst. The pain is so overwhelming that it takes everything I have just to make it through each moment. Crying, calling out, or even cringing in pain would take too much energy. All I can do is focus on my breath, following each inhale and exhale. If you were to see me in that state you might think I looked peaceful.

If you're reading this book you may be in a time of pain, as I was. The migraines hurt, the depression hurts—physical pain is a real symptom of depression along with emotional pain—and the feeling of being cut off from God hurts. You may have prayed for healing as I did but haven't yet received it. I don't know how long your pain will last. I don't know how long the night will be. I don't know why God has gone silent (though some of the mystics I'll quote here give us hints). But I know that God has not abandoned you. God is with you, and not only that, God suffers with you; the same way God suffered with me back then.

Karen Gonzalez offers a broader and deeper perspective on suffering in her book *The God Who Sees*. In it, she writes about her experience as an immigrant. She draws on the biblical story of Joseph, who was sold into slavery in Egypt:

> For Joseph, and for other vulnerable people throughout the world, that question [of why we suffer] may be less complicated than it seems for more privileged people who associate health and wealth with God's love and blessing. For many immigrants and others on the underside of history, God's presence in suffering isn't about complex theological arguments about theodicy or sovereignty or how bad things can happen to good people. For them, God's presence in suffering is what enables them to live. Indeed, for many who suffer, Christ on the cross offers the comfort of knowing that they serve a God who himself has known great sorrow and suffering.[3]

We most likely won't know why, in this life, we experience so much pain. But for me, it helped to know not only that Jesus was suffering with me but that others were sick, weary, and suffering as well. Not because it made the pain any less—and not because I wished pain and suffering on anyone else—but because it helped me feel less alone.

One of my favorite prayers during that time was from Compline, the evening prayer used by various Christian traditions. It's hard to pray a morning prayer when your own night seems to never end. But the evening prayers seemed more manageable. I loved one line in particular:

Keep watch, dear Lord, with those who work, or watch, or weep this night, and give your angels charge over those who sleep. Tend the sick, Lord Christ; give rest to the weary, bless the dying, soothe the suffering, pity the afflicted, shield the joyous; and all for your love's sake. *Amen.*"[4]

This is my prayer for you right now as you read this. I pray that God will soothe your suffering. But until that happens, I pray that God will keep watch with you as you work, or watch, or weep this long night:

Keep watch, dear Christ, with this beloved soul, who weeps and waits, just as you wept and waited in your long night on the cross. Walk with your beloved child through the dark until the morning comes. Amen.

Notes

1. Henri Nouwen, *Turn My Mourning into Dancing* (Nashville: Thomas Nelson, 2001), 11.

2. Heb 4:14–16.

3. Karen Gonzalez, *The God Who Sees*, (Harrisonburg, VA: Herald, 2019), 99.

4. "An Order for Compline," *The Online Book of Common Prayer*, https://tinyurl.com/y6jqynce.

4. Carrying on Until You Can't Carry on Any More

Depression has been roughly divided into small (mild or dysthymic) and large (major) depression. Mild depression is a gradual and sometimes permanent thing that undermines people the way rust weakens iron. It is too much grief at too slight a cause, pain that takes over from the other emotions and crowds them out. Such depression takes up bodily occupancy in the eyelids and in the muscles that keep the spine erect. It hurts your heart and lungs, making the contraction of involuntary muscles harder than it needs to be. . . . Large depression is the stuff of breakdowns. If one imagines a soul of iron that weathers with grief and rusts with mild depression, then major depression is the startling collapse of a whole structure.

~Andrew Solomon[1]

You are doing the damn well best you can.

~My friend Matteo

You may be weary. It's hard to tell just by looking at you. You may be bone-tired with a fatigue that penetrates skin and sinew, heart and liver, down to your marrow. In this type-A world, we all have dark circles under our eyes from waking up early to catch the bus to work, drinking coffee when we get tired instead of resting, taking Advil when we have a headache instead of slowing down. Most of us are weary, searching for rest and restoration.

But you—*you* may have a deeper, iron-rusted weariness that others can't understand. You may have been carrying sorrow for years that weighs you down like sodden clothing and pain that adds extra effort to every movement. You'd think carrying extra weight would strengthen your muscles, that walking through the fire daily would make you fire-proof, but instead your muscles atrophy, and your skin becomes burned and blistered. You don't recover as quickly as others seem to.

Andrew Solomon, in his atlas of depression, *The Noonday Demon*, describes how chronic dysthymic (mild) depression can weaken you over time. Solomon writes, "Mild depression is a gradual and sometimes permanent thing that undermines people the way rust weakens iron. It is too much grief at too slight a cause, pain that takes over from the other emotions and crowds them out."[2]

You may be carrying this weariness, this wearing down of your structural supports, like I did, and you may not even be aware of it. You may think it is normal, that life is supposed to be this hard. You may think this because your parents or other caregivers were also depressed and didn't know it. You may think you're just lazy—or maybe you know you're not, damn it, but other people tell you that you are, and it's hard to argue when you struggle to get out of bed each morning.

FOR RESILIENCE

> My strength is no accident.
> It was planted
> deep in my rich soil
> long before I thought to
> need it.
> This life has already stretched me
> until sore muscles tore.
> I have been made to
> feel so small
> I almost disappeared.
> almost.
> but I keep rising toward the sunshine.
> I am
> deep roots and sharp thorns and
> wide leaves catching light.
> I hold on to this slope
> where rocks slide,
> the earth corrodes,
> seasons change but I remain.
> I take up space
> against all odds.
> The stubborn, savage beauty of one
> who cannot disappear.[3]

Really, you are a miracle of strength, the way you make it through each day and week with rusted bones. It is not surprising that you eventually collapse. It is more surprising that you stayed upright for so long.

The other type of depression, major depression, happens often after years of this so-called mild kind, when you suddenly, often seemingly out of the blue, reach your limit. "Large depression," says Solomon, "is the stuff of breakdowns. If one imagines a soul of iron that weathers with grief and rusts with mild depression, then major depression is the startling collapse of a whole structure."[4]

You may be weary but have never collapsed. You may have collapsed and quickly pulled yourself back together, stuck on spackling and duct tape, and made it to work or to school to pick up your kids, but you never really addressed the collapse or the weariness that led to it.

I see you.

It's difficult to say when the normal sadness and insecurities of life became something more for me. In my work as a nanny, I see children weep despairingly with every ounce of their little beings and then laugh and play moments later with tears still glistening on their cheeks. I remember crying myself to sleep as a child of eight, and ten, and twelve, and waking up in the morning feeling nothing of the devastation that led to those tears. Life often seemed hard and scary, but is it that way for children who aren't going to develop depression, too? I have only my own memories for reference.

I was born to a father who struggled with drug addiction and untreated bipolar disorder for many years. My parents married at the hippy-commune where my dad first got clean and where they both became born-again Christians. Dad was kicked out of the program for sneaking my mom in one night, but when they decided to marry, the commune allowed them to hold the ceremony there.

The first few years of my parents' marriage, and the first few years of my life, were marked by Dad's struggle to recover from addiction and get proper treatment for his bipolar disorder. He was also trying to finish up his bachelor's degree at Brown University. My mom spent many anxious nights alone with a newborn in a basement apartment in Providence, not knowing if or when my dad was coming home.

I have a memory from when my dad was in the hospital, getting treated for bipolar disorder (then called manic-depression). My baby brother and I got to sleep in my mom's bed, a special treat that made Dad's absence less scary. I wanted my mom to sing a song my dad usually sang to us, a Jewish lullaby and resistance song called "Dona Dona," but she did not know the words. I remember, too, standing outside the hospital after we visited him, playing games with cold hands while we waited for our ride. He told me later that he shot up in front of me in the car once, but I don't remember that.

By the time I was four he was sober, medicated, and employed. My parents still struggled, but it felt like things were getting better a little at a time. Still, I remember being anxious often. I was scared of things that made sense and things that didn't—things like my mom dying of cancer, my parents getting a divorce, our house burning down, being in a terrible car accident, finding out I was adopted, losing a limb, or going blind. I would wake up in the middle of the night and tip-toe into my parents' bedroom to make sure they were still breathing. My parents always tried to reassure me, but it seemed to me that because there were so many things that could go terribly wrong in this life, at least one of them was going to happen to us.

When I was eight, my dad started seminary on the North Shore of Massachusetts. We moved into a cozy house in a suburban neighborhood, and I have many happy memories of riding my bike to the library and playing with my brother among the trees in our yard. Around that time, though, I started feeling tired a lot, and generally unwell, but I couldn't explain what was wrong. I would go to the school nurse frequently, and she would take my temperature and send me back to class when it was normal. I now think I was starting to have migraine symptoms—fatigue, nausea, dizziness, and sensitivity to light and noise—but, like my migraines now, they would often present without the actual headache.

Since I was usually at school when I felt ill, my parents thought that I just didn't like school, which was true. I loved learning, but the necessary social interactions were hard for me. I couldn't figure out how the other kids fooled around with each other with such ease. I wanted to be somewhere quiet, reading and getting lost in my imagination. I think I've always been naturally introverted, but it was more than that. The constant stimulation of fluorescent lights, my classmate's noise and confusing interactions, and the teacher's expectations triggered the symptoms that were to become migraines. Sometimes I would ask to go to the bathroom and stay there for as long as I could.

In seventh grade, I started having full-blown migraines often in the evenings after a long day of school. In eight grade and high school, I remember times of feeling really low. In retrospect those times were probably depressive episodes. In high school, I was also taking on a support role for many of my friends. Many of them were struggling with abuse and mental illness, and despite my own depression I was a relatively stable friend to confide in. I dated a boy from a nearby school who, as a teen, began having memories of ritual sexual and physical assault at an early age, and struggled with depression and suicidal thoughts because of them. I just wanted a boyfriend to hold hands with and have my first kiss, but instead I became alternately a therapist and scapegoat. I wish I'd been able to say no to him, to walk away and believe I was worth more than how he treated me. I wish I'd been able to tell the adults in my life what was really going on. I was carrying too much for a seventeen year old.

It was a relief to escape to college and get a clean start. But the depression followed me there too, and the rust of the anxiety, depression, and migraines began to build up and weaken me. I had great times, too, but they always felt precarious, like I knew that the depression was lurking just around the corner like storm clouds at the edge of the sky. Finally, at the beginning of my senior year, a combination of academic stress, romantic troubles, and a botched wisdom tooth extraction triggered a crisis. In Andrew Solomon's words, the soul of iron that had been weathered and rusted collapsed completely. It was my first major depressive episode.

Twelve years later, in the midst of another major depression, I sat in a psychiatrist's office discussing which medication I was going to try next. It was the first time since senior year of college that I'd seen a psychiatrist and been on medication. Since my father has bipolar disorder, my doctor had been extra careful about the medications he tried (antidepressants can trigger manic episodes in someone with latent bipolar disorder). The psychiatrist told me that he didn't think I was bipolar. Instead he diagnosed me with dysthymia with major depressive episodes.

It was the first time I'd heard the word dysthymia, but it made so much sense. The building hadn't just suddenly collapsed out of nowhere. It was weakened over so many years of pushing through pain. It's like when runners collapse at the end of a marathon. Their exhaustion makes sense if you've seen the race. But with depression, it might not be evident from the out-side how much you've endured up till the moment of collapse. You might not even realize it yourself. It takes miles of running hard to get to the point where your body completely shuts down. Many of us have been running hard for years, pushing ourselves to our very limit. We've kept calm and carried on, and now we just can't anymore. Really, it's miraculous that we've made it this far considering all we've been carrying.

Notes

1. Andrew Solomon, *The Noonday Demon* (New York: Scribner, 2001), 17.
2. Solomon, *The Noonday Demon*, 16.
3. Meta Herrick Carlson, *Ordinary Blessings* (Minneapolis: Fortress Press, 2020), 35.
4. Carlson, *Ordinary Blessings,* 17.

5. Learning to Pray When Prayer Hurts

There are all kinds of ways in which God speaks to us—through our thoughts or any one of our faculties. But keep in mind that God's first language is silence.

~Thomas Keating[1]

In Centering Prayer we go beyond thought and image, beyond the senses and the rational mind, to that center of our being where God is working a wonderful work.

~Basil Pennington[2]

I didn't have a particular denomination growing up. We moved around a lot, first as my dad struggled to stay clean and get treatment, and then as he went to seminary and settled into a career as the chaplain at the Maine State Prison. Most of the churches we attended, though, were generally Evangelical—believing in the inerrancy of the Bible and that faith in Jesus was necessary for salvation.

When I was a teenager my parents didn't insist that I attend church with them. Still, I felt a strong personal connection to God, and when I was fifteen years old, I started reading my Bible and praying every night.

Someone had given me a checklist for reading the whole Bible in a year, and I found it so satisfying to check the little box after I'd read my three chapters for the day. As a child I'd always prayed and felt a deep connection to the God I read about in biblical story-books, but this was a new way to pray: Every evening, alone in my room, responding to what I'd read in Scripture. I started writing regularly in my journal at that time, too, phrasing many of my entries as prayer-letters to Jesus. Later, I learned that there was a term in Evangelical circles for what I was doing: A "quiet time."

I kept up my daily reading and prayer throughout high school, college, and seminary, reading the Bible all the way through several times. I sometimes missed days. I wasn't concerned about perfect attendance, but I felt fed by that time with God, studying and talking to God about my day, reveling in the love and presence I felt. When I discovered coffee, my quiet time shifted to the morning. My journals were filled with my prayers, written out as a long, ongoing letter to God.

When I finished my seminary degree I moved into a multi-house Christian community in Boston. I shared a house with a family of five and two other single people. My mornings were suddenly louder and more hectic as I and seven other people all got ready for our days. This made it difficult to get into a contemplative mood. In the evenings, I was starting to feel a strange sadness and loneliness that was at odds with the sense of fellowship and community I had during the day. I found it increasingly hard to pray and find meaning in the words of scripture.

As the months passed, my evening sadness spread

to the nights and mornings, and soon to the whole day. I couldn't sleep, work was stressful, and my migraines were worsening. I couldn't seem to read the Bible anymore without feeling a deep sense of grief at having lost that feeling of connection with God. As the depression worsened and anxiety increased, quiet times went from empty to actively painful. The words that used to nourish me now tasted bitter in my mouth.

But not only had this kind of prayer been my practice for almost two decades, it was the kind prescribed by my church and the parachurch organization where I worked. I was a leader working with students from America and abroad, supposedly teaching specific methods of inductive Bible study and active prayer. I *had* been teaching it, for a long time, and my own practice of an (almost) daily quiet time had inspired others to do the same. I did not want to give it up.

My housemate, Matteo, suggested I try a different kind of prayer. He gave me books by Basil Pennington and Thomas Merton that talked about something called centering prayer. It is a simple way of praying that does not involve speaking, but simply sitting in God's presence. You choose a word or phrase to help you focus, something simple like "peace" or "Jesus." Then, sitting comfortably, you close your eyes, and say the word as you breathe. If you notice your attention wandering, you just gently bring it back.

As I sat and began to breathe, I felt my body relaxing and my restless thoughts quieting. Rather, my thoughts didn't quiet exactly, but in centering prayer, I found a way to move deeper into myself and into God's presence in a way that made the thoughts less important. I imagined my thoughts as clouds passing overhead—I didn't have to attach myself to them, but I didn't have to try to shut them off either. I could simply notice them floating up there, acknowledge them, and then return to the deeper place below, where my spirit was with God.

It felt so good just to be quiet, to feel like I didn't have to try to figure anything out, or to make myself think or feel anything. I didn't feel the same sense of God's presence that I used to, but I felt something quieter and deeper, a trust that God was there whether I felt anything or not. Jeanne Guyon, the mystic who first described this kind of prayer said,

> The Lord is found *only* within your spirit, in the recesses of your being, in the Holy of Holies; this is where He dwells. The Lord once promised to come and make His home within you. (John 14:23) He promised to there meet those who worship Him and who do His will. The Lord *will* meet you in your spirit. It was St. Augustine who once said that he had lost much time in the beginning of his Christian experience by trying to find the Lord outwardly rather than by turning inwardly.[3]

I loved the ideas that in fact God never left me, that the Spirit's home was inside me, that my very being was already in constant prayer and that all I had to do was be still to connect the Spirit.

It was also deeply peaceful to rest in my body. I was consumed with anxious thoughts—the constant worrying and trying to figure out what was wrong and what I needed to do about it, the guilt that I couldn't just get over it and get on with my work and community obligations—that all lived in my head. I was sick of my head. I couldn't turn those thoughts off no matter how hard I tried. But with contemplative prayer it didn't matter. It was like the difference between engaging a troll on the internet and muting him. Or better yet, it was like ignoring him while he went on and on as I sank deeper underground, reaching a place where his voice had no power over me. In my own body, the depths of me, somewhere between my abdomen and my belly, was a sanctuary I'd never imagined. And it was prayer!

While this brought me some comfort, I wasn't yet ready to lay aside the way of relating to God that had served me so well for so many years. My goal wasn't to accept and lean into this new experience, this seeming darkness in which I no longer felt God's presence. My goal was to make it stop, to get better, or to at least understand how long it was likely to last. I equated healing with moving backwards, returning to the way things were. I didn't realize that God had an even deeper healing planned.

Of course, the fact that this next stage in my spiritual journey coincided with a major depressive episode made it incredibly difficult to parse how much of what I was going through was spiritual and how much biological. Depression is an illness, a biological and chemical malfunction, but writers like Jean Guyon were saying that this spiritual experience that seemed to correspond with the depression was a good thing though not an easy one.

> But what happens when that revelation begins to fade away; what do you do when it no longer brings the enjoyment it once did? When this happens, it simply means that God has decided it best to put an end to that experience. What must be your attitude? You must freely yield to having it taken away from you. Lay it aside. The Lord wishes to move on to a deeper and more central understanding of Himself. . . . Learn, having done this, to accept equally all His gifts, whether they are light or darkness."[4]

While I was still working for the Evangelical organization, there wasn't a lot of room to do this inner work. They expected me—and I expected myself—to quickly figure out which medication would make me better so that I could keep practicing and teaching the forms of prayer and worship that had crumbled in my hands. But how could I feed other people sand that I couldn't eat myself?

At a training week in a mid-western college town, we were sent out to practice street evangelism, a practice that always made me deeply uncomfortable. The depression was bad; I was having migraines, which I almost always did in those days, and even ordinary conversation was becoming extremely difficult. I just couldn't do it. I felt angry at the organization and doubtful that my idea of evangelism—open-hearted conversations about God in which I listened as much as

I spoke, and I trusted the Spirit to do the work of converting people—was compatible with what the organization was asking from me.

But I also felt like a failure. If I'd had my old tools of daily Bible reading, and confessional and intercessional prayer, I might have been able to power through the street evangelism to get to the part where the good conversations happened. In fact, I might have been able to power through all the parts of evangelicalism that weren't a good fit for me and were becoming a worse fit as I continued to change despite myself. It was so hard to discern which parts of my evangelizing were difficult because of the depression and migraines, and which were difficult because God was leading me in a different direction. But the blessing of centering prayer was that I could stop trying to figure this all out for a few moments. I could stop thinking at all for those moments, or at least stop latching on to those thoughts. Breathe. Rest. Trust.

Does any of this sound similar to your own experience? God may be removing an old revelation to make way for a new one. Maybe you resent this change and wish you could keep things the way they were. Or maybe you are ready to embrace what God has for you, but you are in a church or other community that may not accept that change.

How would it feel to stop trying to figure everything out, just for a moment? Take a moment to breathe deeply and think of only one word—for example, "peace" or "trust"—or, if it feels better for you, don't think of any words at all. Close your eyes and sink deep into your belly, far from the swirling thoughts in your head. Your mind has been on duty for so long; let it have a few minutes off and trust in your body to take care of you for a change. The path home to your true love is already unobstructed. The doors are already flung wide open, and all you have to do to enter is to breathe.

Notes

1. Thomas Keating, *Open Mind, Open Heart* (New York: Continuum, 1997), 57.

2. Basil Pennington, *Centering Prayer* (Garden City, NY: Image, 1982), 18.

3. Jean Guyon, *Experiencing the Depths of Jesus Christ* (Jacksonville, FL: SeedSowers, 1975), 11.

4. Guyon, *Experiencing the Depths of Jesus Christ*, 43.

6. Prayer and the Body

Become the witness. Becoming the witness does not mean pushing [our emotion] away; it means allowing it fully, giving it all our attention and awareness but without believing it is what we are. The emotion takes place in us, yes, and you may even say it's part of us, but it is not who we truly are, and seeing that frees us to be able to fully experience an emotion—and when we are able to fully experience an emotion it will change, because the nature of life is that sooner or later everything changes.

Feel the raw feeling. When we resist an emotion, it tends to persist. Also, when we believe in an emotion and in the story of why it should be there, we tend to keep fueling it, and it will linger and come back. But when we can feel the raw feeling, the emotion in the body, without getting involved in any stories about why and how, that is when the emotion loses its grip on us and changes.

~Esther Ekhart[1]

After I'd been doing centering prayer for a while, I had an opportunity to observe for myself that it was actually having a physical impact as well as mental. My neurologist suggested a treatment for the migraines called biofeedback, which she had seen produce excellent results. I went to the first session not knowing what to expect, but as Dr. Joshua Wootton, a kind, bearded psychologist, began to explain it to me, I exclaimed, "That sounds like centering prayer!" It turned out that he was also a practitioner of centering prayer, and he had been involved in a workshop related to the practice with none other than my beloved writer, Henri Nouwen.

Though I had been sent there for migraine pain, the treatment was relevant to my depression as well. Writing for *Boston Magazine*, Dr. Wootton explained it this way: "Pain frequently accompanies depression. . . . There is a highly intertwined and overlapping relationship between depression and chronic pain."[2] During my biofeedback session, I was hooked up to instruments that would monitor my heartrate, body temperature, amount of sweat, and other bodily functions while I engaged in a meditation that was almost like centering prayer, without, of course, the religious element.

Afterwards, Dr. Wootton and I went over the collected data and reviewed the physiological effects that the meditation had on my body. This is a great way to learn how to regulate the body's autonomic nervous system, the system that is triggered in the fight or flight response. After several sessions of biofeedback, I would have the skills to choose a "relaxation response"—to deliberately calm my body's physiology, and the "fight and flight" reaction that exacerbated my pain. The same process that helped me connect to God could help minimize the migraines, as well as anxiety. As Dr. Wootton writes:

> Meditation, by contrast [to chronic pain], elicits a unique, wakeful or conscious hypometabolic integrated state in which the organism is even more deeply at rest than during sleep. Deep meditation can reduce cortisol secretion, oxygen consumption, and blood lactate levels and increase the secretion of hormones such as serotonin and melatonin. . . . With acute pain, the fight or flight response can motivate the organism towards preservation, but with chronic pain the response becomes obsolete, actually precipitating deterioration in normal pain processing and contributing toward exacerbations and persistence of pain, as well as poor pain tractability. By eliciting the relaxation response, mediation can be characterized as reasserting parasympathetic dominance, or at least, balance, calming and relating the musculoskeletal system and adjusting the hormonal milieu and pain neurotransmission to a less urgent, excitatory, and preoccupying framework.[3]

(For those of you who want to dig deeper into the science behind all this, I put a longer excerpt from that article in the endnotes.)

Years later, I had a similar experience when I started doing yoga. The first time I went to a yoga class I struggled, and I watched the clock the entire time. I knew the class was an hour and fifteen minutes, so it was with a sense of surprised relief that I realized, with twenty minutes still to go, we were winding down. The poses became slower and easier, and then the teacher told us to lie on our backs and make ourselves comfortable. She suggested putting on our socks and covering ourselves with blankets. While we did that, she dimmed the lights, put on soft, meditative music, and I suddenly realized it was nap time! Just like in kindergarten, we all lay together on our mats and rested. It felt funny lying in such an intimate, vulnerable position in a roomful of people. We closed our eyes as the teacher led us through a relaxation exercise. I soon forgot about the others and reveled in the peace and quiet as I rested my sore muscles and settled my anxious mind.

Savasana is the word both for the pose—on your back with your arms out at a slight angle—and the accompanying relaxation exercise. It happens at the end of many yoga classes and is a way of allowing the poses you have just done to settle into your mind and muscles. As in centering prayer and biofeedback, you are encouraged to take a passive attitude to your thoughts, to allow them to exist without trying to change them, latching on to them, or identifying with them.

One analogy used in centering prayer is to see your thoughts as clouds going overhead. You notice them, but they don't affect you down where you are, and they blow past with the wind. For someone who has struggled with anxiety, this is incredibly powerful. I don't have to try to STOP thinking the anxious thoughts, or to change them or replace them with positive thoughts—exercises which left me exhausted and twice as stressed out—but I don't have to define myself by them, either. I can nod at them, even greet them with friendly acknowledgement and send them on their way.

I sometimes use that imagery of clouds passing above. Sometimes I imagine my thoughts as a physical object beside me—there, but not a part of me. Observe your thoughts, my yoga teacher, Esther Ekhart, says, acknowledge them without trying to change them. So I notice: *I am angry at my housemate for something stupid; I am worried about money; my back hurts.* It's okay. I don't have to try to stop being angry right now, or stop worrying, or get my back pain to stop. That's just how I feel. It's not me. My true self, which is deeper than those thoughts and feelings, is at peace.

Because of my particular Christian upbringing, I spent a lot of time thinking about sin. I now believe that many of the things I thought were sins were actually just the varying thoughts and emotions of young-adulthood, just me struggling to figure out, to understand, myself and the world around me. I tried to change my thoughts and feelings, to avoid being conflicted or confused. The Hebrew word for repentance, *shuv*, means turning away from bad choices and back toward good, rejecting the wrong path and turning to the right one, turning back to God. I still find that imagery helpful at times. But I wish that I had known about Savasana, too. I wish I could have given myself that space and gentleness to not immediately define my feelings as sins and to not identify myself with them. Repenting of anger never helped me let go of that anger. But when I gently acknowledge it, place it next to me, and quiet my body and my mind, I can let it go.

****

One evening last August, after a long day at work, I came home and made my way to my yoga mat. During Savasana, I opened my eyes and looked up at the ceiling, and I noticed something I never had before. Above, the pale, textured ceiling was bordered by dark wood paneling that matched the wood on the walls, and it created a framed rectangle the exact size of my living room. My living room is the place I spend more waking time than any other room. It's where I work and play on my computer, read, watch TV, entertain guests, and do yoga. The living room is the space most full of me, my activities, and my presence. And that night, I noticed that there is a space the exact same size and shape above it. It is my living room, but it is emptied of furniture, rugs, house plants, computers, tissues, candles—all the things that clutter the floor below. It is a framed, empty canvas, in the shape of my life, my living, my room.

It occurred to me that this space perfectly represents the place we go when we meditate, do centering prayer, or lie in Savasana. In this case the clutter is down below, and that beautiful, clear, uncluttered space is above—exactly the shape of us, of our lives, but empty of all of the thoughts and anxieties, habits and coping mechanisms, that make up our daily lives. It is a blank canvas where we can meet God and create something together. God is the paint, and we are the brush, or we are the brush and God is the artist, or we are only the canvas and God is all the rest: The blended colors of the full spectrum, the rocky pigment sparkling in the paint, the sharp edge of the palette knife, the rough horse-hair of the brush, and the Artist Herself, waiting for her materials to settle down, to move all that clutter off of the canvas so she can finally begin.

****

You might need a referral from your doctor to do biofeedback, but centering prayer and yoga are more readily accessible. At the end of the book, I give suggestions for further reading about centering prayer, as well as the link to my favorite online yoga classes. But you can begin the process right now by closing your eyes and taking a deep breath. Accept any thoughts and feelings you have in this moment, without trying to change them. Even feelings that are often seen as negative—fear, anger, sadness, despair. Allow them to sit next to you, or to float above you like clouds. They are real, but they do not define you. Your true self is deeper, entirely seen, accepted, and loved by the God that created you.

Notes

1. Esther Ekhart, "Yoga and Emotional pain," *Ekhart Yoga*, https://tinyurl.com/y6qwxf4z.

2. Beth Israel and Deaconess Medical Center, "Depression and Pain Go Hand in Hand," *Boston Magazine*, https://tinyurl.com/y57nsxnf.

3. Joshua Wooton, "Meditation and Chronic Pain," in *Integrative Pain Medicine: The Science and Practice of Complementary and and Alternative Medicine in Pain Management*, ed. Joseph F. Audette and Allison Bailey (Totowa, NJ: Humana, 2008) 201. The experience of acute pain has in immediate impact upon the sympathetic nervous system. Heart and respiratory rates, blood pressure, blood glucose levels, and muscle tension all increase, as the adrenal cortex activates the stress response with glucocorticoids that elicit the "fight or flight" response. When pain goes unrelieved, however, and is unresponsive to medical care, enduring beyond its usefulness as a signal to action, then it may be said to have become chronic and indicative of changes in the way the brain processes pain. The experience of chronic pain leads to changes in the subjective apprehension of pain, heightening responsiveness to pain stimuli and making the individual more susceptible to exacerbations with the trigger of psychological anticipation, giving rise to comorbid anxiety, fear, and ultimately, depression. In these circumstances, the threshold of pain is lowered, resulting from the depletion of serotonin and endorphin levels, while other hormonal responses, like the release of cortisol, are heightened and prolonged, increasing the deleterious impact of stress on the body.

    Meditation, by contrast [to chronic pain], elicits a unique, wakeful or conscious hypometabolic integrated state in which the organism is even more deeply at rest than during sleep. Deep meditation can reduce cortisol secretion, oxygen consumption, and blood lactate levels and increase the secretion of hormones such as serotonin and melatonin. Until relatively recently, the principal working hypothesis of how meditation, in particular the relaxation response and mindfulness meditation, exerts its therapeutic physiological influence was that, by reducing sympathetic arousal and increasing the activity of the parasympathetic nervous system, it moderates the impact of the fight or flight response. With acute pain, the fight or flight response can motivate the organism towards preservation, but with chronic pain the response becomes obsolete, actually precipitating deterioration in normal pain processing and contributing toward exacerbations and persistence of pain, as well as poor pain tractability. By eliciting the relaxation response, mediation can be characterized as reasserting parasympathetic dominance, or at least, balance, calming and relating the musculoskeletal system and adjusting the hormonal milieu and pain neurotransmission to a less urgent, excitatory, and preoccupying framework.

Recent research has suggested more complex mechanisms through which meditation may affect chronic pain and has provided a number of correctives with regard to earlier hypotheses. Recent studies of the neural basis of meditation focusing on hypothalamic and autonomic nervous system changes, as well as autonomic cortical activity, have pointed to sharp increases in vasoconstrictor arginine vasopressin, resulting in decreased fatigue among meditators, as well as heightened arousal. Research now indicates a mutual activation of the parasympathetic and sympathetic systems during mediation as eliciting a sense of profound calmness, as well as alertness and during meditation, as opposed to the original view of parasympathetic dominance, consistent with a balanced autonomic response that is, in turn, consistent with subjective descriptions of meditation as eliciting a sense of profound calmness, as well as alertness and attunement (Wooton, "Meditation and Chronic Pain," 201).

7. Monsters Under the Bed

We can surely no longer pretend that our children are growing up in a peaceful, secure, and civilized world. We've come to the point where it's irresponsible to try to protect them from the irrational world they will have to live in when they grow up. The children themselves haven't yet isolated themselves by selfishness and indifference; they do not fall easily into the error of despair; they are considerably braver than most grownups. Our responsibility to them is not to pretend that if we don't look, evil will go away, but to give them weapons against it.

~Madeleine L'Engle[1]

When I was a child, I lived in my head. I read stories and wrote myself into those stories as an important character, helping to save the day. I was Fiver's confidante and Hazel's advisor in *Watership Down*. I walked with *Julie of the Wolves* through the frozen tundra. As I became older, my worlds expanded: I was an orphaned empath in *Star Trek the Next Generation*. I was friends with John Lennon and Davy Jones of The Monkees. I spent hours in those worlds, creating witty dialogue and orchestrating intense moments where I battled evil or gave up my powers to save a friend. I looked forward to nighttime when I could lie in bed for a half-hour or so before sleep, building on yesterday's scenes, escaping into one or another of my secret worlds.

At some point in my twenties I decided it was probably time to give up these worlds. They weren't doing any harm, but it seemed like I should give up that childhood habit in order to be a mature adult. So I quit, cold turkey. But I found there were fantasies that stayed with me, similar in some ways to the ones I enjoyed as a child, but scarier. I would find myself imagining scenarios where I was seriously injured, attacked, or raped, but I heroically survived, and my friends gathered round me to celebrate my survival. Sometimes I would imagine one of my parents tragically dying and me having to learn to live with that terrible grief.

When I was babysitting, I would picture a car coming around the corner and striking the child, forcing me to do desperately perform CPR even though I knew it was too late. The thoughts were brief, but so intense that my heart would start racing, my breath would catch, and my anxiety spike. One moment I was fine, and the next I was panicked, trying to bring my thoughts back to the present.

It wasn't until much later that I learned these thoughts were part of the depression. Psychiatrists call them psychotic depression, or delusional depression, but those terms can be misleading. I never lost touch with reality. I didn't think those things were really happening. But my body reacted as if they were. Biofeedback is really helpful in these cases, teaching my body that it's possible to respond to intense thoughts not with fight or flight, but calmness. Deep breaths. Touching the things around me, my own warm skin, my friend's shoulder. The things I'm imagining may happen, but they are not happening right now.

Still, there's a reality behind these waking nightmares and the sleeping ones as well. Terrible things do happen. My parents will die one day, and I will likely be alive to grieve them. When I was a child, my parents told me the bad things I feared wouldn't happen, but now I know that's not true. Every day children lose their parents to death or abandonment. It's not delusional to be aware that somewhere in the world children are dying or are shot by the police because of the color of their skin or are taken away from their parents because of a country's horrific refugee policy.

Madeleine L'Engle, another of my beloved companions along the road, said, "We can surely no longer pretend that our children are growing up into a peaceful, secure, and civilized world. We've come to the point where it's irresponsible to try to protect them from the irrational world they will have to live in when they grow up."[2] We tell our children there are no monsters and that they are safe, but there are monsters, and we know it. What we really mean is that the monsters will likely pick some other place to wreak havoc today. We mean we are safe-ish, probably, for now, and the only way to stay sane is to live in denial about the –ish. Some of us are just bad at the denial. If I were in charge, I would call it non-delusional depression. I'd call it paying attention.

But we do have to live our lives, and depression makes it very hard to keep moving, to keep putting one foot in front of the other. Just being aware of all the pain in your own life, in your friends' and family's lives, and in the world altogether tends to make you want to curl up into a ball and cry. And the problem with this, besides the fact that you are not really enjoying your one wild and precious life, is that you may actually be one of the people who can *do* something about someone else's pain and suffering. Your awareness of it may not only be a mental illness, a bleak descriptor penned in your chart in the sharp, quick script of an over-scheduled psychiatrist. It may be a call to action. Because you have to be able to see the monsters in order to fight them. You have to be willing to admit that the emperor has no clothes before you can try to clothe him.

But having your eyes open to the reality of evil in the world is only half of living in reality. You have to see something else, too. You have to see the beauty. You have to see the angels, the good, the God. Depression shows you your own pain and the pain of the world in stark reality, but it hides the very real beauty and tremendous love that also exist in you and all around you.

I have learned ways to bring my thoughts back from those negative fixations. One is deep, slow breathing to calm my body's autonomic nervous system—the fight or flight response. Another is to reach out to friends with a phone call or text. A third is to ground myself in my body's senses. I try to notice my current surroundings in every detail. What do I see, feel, smell, hear? Who am I with? If I can physically touch someone, that helps a lot; if not, touching my own body helps—running my fingers through my hair, lacing my hands together, or raising my arms in the first stretch of a sun-salutation.

One summer afternoon, I was swimming at Walden Pond, having bundled myself out of bed, miraculously fighting depression's despair and heaviness for a few hours. The quiet and solitude lulled me into my own thoughts. Suddenly, I realized my thoughts had left the blue-green swirl of water and sky and had wandered into anxious fantasy. *What if I drowned here,* I thought, and suddenly I was vividly imagining myself drowning. My body responded—my started heart beating faster, and my eyesight began to blur and shift into tunnel vision. It all happened so quickly I didn't have time to prevent it, but once I recognized what was happening, I began my grounding work, forcing my thoughts back to my body and its surroundings. *Where are you right now?* I asked myself. *What are you doing right now? Pay attention. Describe it. What do you know to be true?*

I breathed deep breaths, filling my lungs, and noticed that my body rose softly in the water with the buoyancy of that fresh air inside me. I observed that the sun was warm but the water cool. I saw that I shared my particular cove with a large turtle that had poked its head out of the water in a little triangle, assessing which way I was likely to go so it could go in the opposite direction. Later I sat on my towel, letting the breeze dry me and feeling that breeze raise each of the tiny hairs on my arms. I walked further down the beach and coming around a bend found a cairn in the shallow water, a miracle of architecture, made of stones balanced on sand, rising out of the water. I read a text from a friend asking for prayer, and I prayed for her and asked her to pray for me too. Another friend checked in with a brief message on Facebook. I was surrounded by love.

The monsters are real, but all of this is real, too. In L'Engle's *A Wrinkle in Time*, the angel-like characters, Mrs. Who, Mrs. Which, and Mrs. Whatsit, take the children to space to show them the Darkness, a demonic Thing that is threatening the universe and encroaching upon the earth and many other worlds as well. It is huge and horrible and terrifying.

"The Darkness seemed to seethe and writhe. Was this meant to comfort them?"

But then they see something else:

> Suddenly there was a great burst of light through the Darkness. The light spread out and where it touched the Darkness the Darkness disappeared. The light spread until the patch of Dark Thing had vanished, and there was only a gentle shining and through the shining came the stars, clear and pure. Then, slowly, the shining dwindled until it, too, was gone, and there was nothing but stars and starlight. No shadows. No fear. Only the stars and the clear darkness of space, quite different from the fearful darkness of the Thing. . . .
>
> "It was a star," Mrs. Whatsit said sadly. "A star giving up its life in battle with the Thing."[3]

The monsters are real, but the stars are real, too. There is great evil and sadness in the world, but there are also stars and the clear, good darkness of space. The star that gave its life in the book was fiction, of course, but there are real acts of love and healing every day. My swim through the glacier-dug pond was one. My prayer for my friend as we texted each other that we were struggling was one, and so was hers for me. The act of building the cairn was one too. Any creative act is.

And as I looked through my pictures from my trip to Walden, I remembered that a cairn can be a memorial, too. Maybe its maker was a star. Maybe she was carrying the weight of the world's grief, past and future, and shaped it into the best thing she could, a piece of art. Maybe she knew that the monsters were real because she had to fight one of the scariest ones just to make it out of the house to fling her art out against them, a star into the night.

The lies that depression tells are powerful because they begin with truth. As a monster itself, depression surrounds you with nothing but monsters while it blocks out the memory of love, and hope, and the sacrificial acts of the stars. We have to keep paying attention, and keep looking for hope and beauty. The night may be long, but only in the darkness can we watch for falling stars, until the day that our own star, the sun, finds us again in the long-delayed dawn.

Hold on. Keep breathing. Each breath is an act of hope and a strike against the monsters. Breathe deep, and feel the buoyancy of your lungs holding you afloat.

Notes

1. Madeleine L'Engle, *A Circle of Quiet* (New York: Farrar, Straus & Giroux, 1972), 99.
2. L'Engle, *A Circle of Quiet*, 99.
3. Madeleine L'Engle, *A Wrinkle in Time*, (New York: Farrar, Straus & Giroux, 1962), 102–3.

8. A Safe Place to Cry While You Learn How Not to Cry

The Welcoming Prayer

Welcome, welcome, welcome.
I welcome everything that comes to me today
because I know it's
for my healing.
I welcome all thoughts, feelings, emotions, per-
sons,
situations, and conditions.
I let go of my desire for power and control.
I let go of my desire for affection, esteem,
approval and pleasure.
I let go of my desire for survival and security.
I let go of my desire to change any situation,
condition, person or myself.
I open to the love and presence of God and
God's action within. Amen.

~Thomas Keating[1]

When I was recovering from that last major depressive episode, I was seeing a spiritual director I really liked. Then one day, at the end of one of our sessions, she said, "I want to note that this is the first time I've seen you that you didn't cry, and to affirm you for that." I was devastated. All day, every day, I was struggling to get through my daily interactions without tears, to hold it together so as not to subject people to my intense depression. I thought I'd found a safe space to cry, but now it felt like I hadn't, not really. I actually think if I'd told her that those words hurt me and why, she would have understood, but I was too discouraged. Plus, I was paying out of pocket to see her, and my bills were adding up. I never went back.

I have always had a deep need to express my feelings and to be acknowledged and comforted. I think this is true for most people. Even a few simple words mean a lot to me; words like, "Wow, that sounds hard," or "I'm sorry you're going through that." I don't want to dwell on my pain, but depression and migraines together create a lot of pain. Depression alone can hurt like hell—physically as well as emotionally. Any kind of solution that skips over the acknowledgement and grieving of that pain is not going to bring real healing for me.

On the other hand, some people might like to just skip ahead to where the pain ends. I can understand that. But in case you're like me, I want to acknowledge what you're going through and what you've been through. It's okay to be overwhelmed. It's okay to cry from pain, from exhaustion, or from fear. Your tears do not mean that you aren't trying hard enough or that you're not open to healing. Life is hard. Life is hard for everyone, but it is hard for you in this particular way at this particular moment. It's okay to feel that pain and express it. There is room for both grieving and healing.

I've discovered that I need to go through three steps in coping with the pain of depression and chronic illness. Of course, progress is never linear, and I've found myself moving between these three steps at various times. Nevertheless, there is a general pattern which I find helpful. First, I need to acknowledge and grieve the pain; next, I need to accept it; and finally, after the first two stages, I will be in a place that allows me to work on treatment or coping mechanisms.

I can't do anything with or about my pain without first acknowledging and grieving it. It hurts, and it's incredibly discouraging that such pain is a part of my daily life. This stage took a lot of time, partly because the pain was so intense and partly because I struggled to find places where it was okay simply to grieve without people expecting me to move on to healing. Now that I know I have this need, I am better able communicate it to friends and family, housemates, and therapists. Some people may not understand, and some may want to be there for me but just don't have the energy or the space or the level of health in their own lives, and that's okay. Ultimately, I needed to create this space for myself, and to stop pushing myself and judging myself for my weakness.

Alia Joy describes a similar kind of acknowledgement in her book, *Glorious Weakness*. She is talking about the biblical character Naomi, who had lost not only her loved ones but any means of supporting herself. Alia is struck by Naomi's honesty in expressing her heartbreak.

I remember reading the book of Ruth as a new Christian, and I came to the verse where Naomi says, "The LORD's hand has turned against me" (1:13 NIV). I thought, *You can't talk to God like that*. . . . Wouldn't it have been a more powerful story if she was widowed and lost both of her sons and was a destitute foreigner, but she told Ruth not to worry because God was faithful and would provide for them? Wouldn't the steadfast thing have been to tell Ruth that God is good and they had nothing to worry about?

I didn't understand it then, but years later, when I had endured a different measure of grief, loss, and suffering, I saw something different. I saw a woman who didn't stop praying even when her words were bitter. . . . Naomi . . . acts in faith even though her heart is broken and frustrated. She is achingly honest about her emptiness and need. God wanted her lament to bind her to him.[2]

Naomi doesn't try to skip ahead to accepting her fate or moving on. She is in pain and she says so. Just like me, she needed space for acknowledgement and lament. And just like Naomi, my pain was real though its source was different—hers from death and loss, and mine from depression and migraines as well as from wounds others had inflicted on me and those I had inflicted on myself. Your own pain may have a different source, but it is still real.

After grieving, though, I needed to find a place of acceptance. This is where centering prayer helped me. The process of acknowledging my thoughts and feelings without getting attached to them helped me to acknowledge and accept my level of health on any given day. I began to accept that, for whatever reason, these were the circumstances I had to work with. On a spiritual level, this meant accepting that God was still present in my life even if I had no sense of God's presence. Striving to find God in the ways I used to, or to remake my life into how it used to be, only prevents me from seeing how God is present and at work in the here and now. Thomas Keating's "Welcoming Prayer," which is quoted at the beginning of this chapter, is one tool to move into this acceptance. He writes,

> Welcoming Prayer is the practice that actively lets go of thoughts and feelings that support the false-self system. It embraces painful emotions experienced in the body rather than avoiding them or trying to suppress them. It does not embrace the suffering as such but the presence of the Holy Spirit in the particular pain, whether physical, emotional, or mental. Thus, it is the full acceptance of the content of the present moment. [In] giving the experience over to the Holy Spirit, the false-self system is gradually undermined and the true self liberated.[3]

And lastly, it's only when I've moved through both grieving and accepting that I can move on to working on ways to manage the pain and to think about restructuring my thoughts and feelings so I can function better. "Don't cry," is never a helpful suggestion for me (is it for you?), but if we start with, "Go ahead and cry, you certainly have reason to," then I will be ready to hear, "Let's think of ways we can help you so your sorrow isn't so debilitating."

One of the ways I learned to manage the pain is a type of therapy called cognitive behavior therapy, or CBT. Cognitive behavioral therapy, "is a form of psychotherapy that treats problems and boosts happiness by modifying dysfunctional emotions, behaviors, and thoughts."[4] I haven't been formally treated by a CBT therapist, but I have found several CBT exercises to be helpful. CBT uses the idea of "cognitive distortions"—ways that our thinking can become stuck and prevent us from grasping the reality of a situation. "Filtering" is a common distortion for those with depression; we filter out the good and beautiful and see only the evil and ugly. My friend once told me that when his depression is bad, he can drive on a beautiful mountain highway, on a glorious summer day, and all he will see is the dead squirrel on the side of the road. Other cognitive distortions include polarized or black and white thinking, overgeneralizations, jumping to conclusions, and catastrophizing:

Polarized Thinking / "Black and White" Thinking

This cognitive distortion is all about seeing black and white only, with no shades of grey. This is all-or-nothing thinking, with no room for complexity or nuance. If you don't perform perfectly in some area, then you may see yourself as a total failure instead of simply unskilled in one area.

Overgeneralization

Overgeneralization is taking a single incident or point in time and using it as the sole piece of evidence for a broad general conclusion. For example, a person may be on the lookout for a job but have a bad interview experience; instead of brushing it off as one bad interview and trying again, they conclude that they are terrible at interviewing and will never get a job offer.

Jumping to Conclusions

Similar to overgeneralization, this distortion involves faulty reasoning in how we make conclusions. Instead of overgeneralizing one incident, however, jumping to conclusions refers to the tendency to be sure of something without any evidence at all. We may be convinced that someone dislikes us with only the flimsiest of proof, or we may be convinced that our fears will come true before we have a chance to find out.

Catastrophizing / Magnifying or Minimizing

This distortion involves expectations that the worst will happen or has happened, based on a slight incident that is nowhere near the tragedy that it is made out to be. For example, you may make a small mistake at work and be convinced that it will ruin the project you are working on, your boss will be furious, and you will lose your job. Alternatively, we may minimize the importance of positive things, such as an accomplishment at work or a desirable personal characteristic.[5]

I was often prone to catastrophizing, which played out mostly in my relationships. If anyone said anything negative to me, or even gave me a less than enthusiastic response to a question, I would lie awake all night, terrified that I'd lost that friendship forever or, worse, that they'd never really liked me and now I finally knew. In fact, 99 percent of the time the person was probably just tired, or distracted, or possibly even a bit annoyed, but our friendship was never in danger.

Cognitive behavioral therapy offers various tools and exercises to help you identify cognitive distortions you may be experiencing and replace them with positive, helpful thoughts. Some exercises focus on identifying and addressing the distortions directly, while others are breathing or muscle relaxation techniques that operate on the same premise as biofeedback. They train your body's autonomic nervous system to remain calm rather than responding to adrenaline-fueled thoughts that cause you to fight or flee. These were things I definitely needed.

****

One night in August, a couple of years after I'd learned some of these techniques, my mom and I went out to stargaze and catch any stragglers from the Perseid meteor shower. We had missed the peak days because of work, and illness, and all the other everyday reasons a person misses beautiful, special things like meteor showers. Still, we decided that we would go out when we could and see what we could see.

I was doing much better with the depression and

anxiety, but going out after dark was still a trigger for me, and one of my go-to fears—my "catastrophizing," to use CBT's language—was that something horrible would happen to my parents. Being alone is when I feel the most calm and safe. Being with others adds to the pressure of needing to appear calm so that I don't either scare them or ruin their experience, or, perhaps my worst fear, make them feel like I'm a drama queen who needs constant attention. These worries exacerbate my initial anxiety. But it's important to learn to work through these feelings and even learn how the presence of others can help in the grounding process.

On this particular summer night, the sky was cooperating with our plan, more or less—a bit hazy with some scattered clouds, but already through the car window, I could see more stars than I was used to seeing in Boston. We drove around New Hampshire's back streets for a while, but there were too many trees. We then drove through the campus of Saint Anselm College, which was so well-lit it made me wonder whether the college had added extra lamp posts because of violent attacks against young women walking at night. I stopped and noticed my thoughts and my increasing heartbeat, and took a deep breath. *You don't have to think about things like that right now*, I told myself; *It's okay. Breathe deeply and think about what is actually happening*. I touched my mom's arm next to me in the car, bare and warm in a tank top, and used it to ground my thoughts in the moment. How easily I move out of time, into thoughts and feelings, both pleasant and unpleasant. *You are here, now*, I told myself. Be here.

We drove for maybe a half an hour when my mom

remembered that there was a new section to the cemetery being prepared—a field dug out and planted with grass seed, waiting for new residents. I countered thoughts of death before they could even set in: *You're here, now, and your mom is here. You're alive.* We pulled over, took a blanket out of the trunk, and made our way carefully around the fence and into the empty field. A single cricket greeted us by the gate.

"I see an animal," I said, grabbing my mother's arm. "I think it's a skunk." I could clearly see the glint of its eyes and the black and white pattern as it wobbled toward us. "Where?" my mom asked, and I took the flashlight from her and pointed it toward . . . a small piece of white wood. No eyes, no movement. Just white next to the black of the night. "Okay," I said, "I have an overactive imagination."

We picked our way carefully down the road and into the field, then we spread out the blanket and lay down, waiting for our eyes to adjust to the light. We lay quietly for a while, watching the sky. I tried not to think of cars going by, of people, of whether it was entirely safe for us to be out here alone at ten-thirty at night. We didn't know which direction to look in, so we gazed upward and tried to be aware of the periphery of our vision as well. After a few minutes we started to chat, catching up on our lives, talking about God and church and our struggles with finding our place. Suddenly my mom said,

"There's one!"

"Aw, I didn't see it," I responded.

And a few minutes later, in unison, "Look, I saw one!" Then a few more, all short and not very bright. We realized they were all toward the north, near the big and little dipper, so we got up and turned our blanket toward Canada. Pine trees rimmed the horizon, and the edge star of the big dipper began to sink below the trees. I imagined the bowl of the dipper filling up with pine sap.

"None of these are very impressive," I said to my mom.

"No," she said.

"Come on, sky!" I exclaimed, "Give us some nice big ones!"

Then I laughed and said, cajolingly,

"Come on, little meteors! Come hang out with us here. The atmosphere is fun, I promise. Nice and warm—it won't burn you up, really." We laughed.

A little while later, I said, "The dew's out, and the blanket's damp. And I'm starting to get a little cold and tired."

"Okay, sky," my mom said, "We want to see three big ones, and then we'll go home."

We chatted a little more, but we didn't talk much about the hard stuff. Dad just got a walker, but for now he's still able to go to the jails and do the ministry he loves. Mom's job is hard, but she needs it for the health insurance. We're not really sure what will happen next, when they'll need to move to a place without stairs, or how much longer Mom can do her job before it gets too hard.

Even before Dad got sick, I used to worry about my parents constantly. It helped a lot to work through my thought patterns with breathing exercises and CBT exercises. Ultimately the truth is that I can't prevent bad things from happening despite my constant worry. It adds nothing to the future; it only takes away joy from the present.

So, be here now, I reminded myself, *under the stars with your real, living, mother. Enjoy this time. There will be time tomorrow to talk about wheelchairs and handicap accessible apartments.* So we talked about poetry and prayer, about our friends, about the constellations and the falling stars.

"Okay, God," my mom said, "I'm going to count to ten, and if there's not a really big one we're going home. One . . . two . . . three . . ." She slowed down as she approached ten, allowing extra time for God's recalcitrance.

"Ten," she said, and her voice was so calm and certain that I was a little surprised when nothing happened. We waited for a few more minutes, anyway, and then helped each other up, picked up the damp blanket and walked easily back to the car, now that our eyes had adjusted to the night.

****

One helpful CBT exercise is a thought record, a template to record your thoughts and reactions to them. Can you think of a recent situation—similar to my stargazing trip with my mom—where you have had overwhelming thoughts or feelings that made it difficult to focus on the moment? For example, mine were thoughts of sexual assault triggered by the lamps on the college campus, fear of the dark (or what the dark might be hiding), and anxiety about my dad's illness.

Dr. Steven M. Melemis offers these seven questions to help you process your experience and learn to understand your thoughts and feelings while also helping you learn how to manage your reactions.

1. The situation: Briefly describe the situation that led to your unpleasant feelings. This will help you remember the situation later if you review your notes.
2. Initial thought: What thought first crossed your mind? This was probably a subconscious or automatic thought that you have had before.
3. Consider the consequences: Why do you want to change this thinking? What will be the consequences if you don't change? Look at the psychological, physical, professional, and relationship consequences.
4. Challenge your initial thought: How successful has this thinking been for you in the past? What facts do you have that support or challenge your initial thought? What strengths do you have that you may have overlooked? What advice would you give someone else in the same situation?
5. [Optional] Negative thinking: Summarize the kind of negative thinking behind your initial thought. Identify one or more of the basic types of negative thinking: All-or-nothing, Focusing on the negatives, Catastrophizing, Negative self-labelling, Mind reading, Should statements.
6. [Optional] Background: When did you first have initial thoughts like this? How deep do the roots go? Do you know anyone else who thinks like this?

How successful has this thinking been for them?

7. Alternative thinking: Now that you understand your negative thinking, how could you have handled the situation differently? Drop any negative assumptions, and think of possibilities or facts that you may have overlooked.[6]

Notes

1. Thomas Keating, "The Welcoming Prayer," The Work of the People, https://tinyurl.com/y42tcezm.

2. Alia Joy, *Glorious Weakness* (Grand Rapids: Baker, 2019), 152–53.

3. Thomas Keating, "The Welcoming Prayer," Contemplative Outreach, https://tinyurl.com/yy3j9nug.

4. "Cognitive Behavioral Therapy," *Psychology Today*, https://tinyurl.com/y8v2gel7.

5. Courtney Ackerman, "25 CBT Techniques and Worksheets for Cognitive Behavioral Therapy," *Positive Psychology*, March 20, 2017, https://tinyurl.com/ybkd7tm9.

6. Steven M. Melemis, "CBT Worksheet—Cognitive Therapy Thought Record," I Want to Change My Life, last modified October 4, 2018, https://tinyurl.com/y2e8h4rt.

9. Darkness and Light

"Darkness" is shorthand for anything that scares me — that I want no part of — either because I am sure that I do not have the resources to survive it or because I do not want to find out. The absence of God is in there, along with the fear of dementia and the loss of those nearest and dearest to me. So is the melting of polar ice caps, the suffering of children, and the nagging question of what it will feel like to die. If I had my way, I would eliminate everything from chronic back pain to the fear of the devil from my life and the lives of those I love — if I could just find the right night-lights to leave on.

At least I think I would. The problem is this: when, despite all my best efforts, the lights have gone off in my life (literally or figuratively, take your pick), plunging me into the kind of darkness that turns my knees to water, nonetheless I have not died. The monsters have not dragged me out of bed and taken me back to their lair. The witches have not turned me into a bat. Instead, I have learned things in the dark that I could never have learned in the light, things that have saved my life over and over again, so that there is really only one logical conclusion. I need darkness as much as I need light.

~Barbara Brown Taylor[1]

I've chosen to speak of my own experience with depression as a long night, an extended time of darkness. But nighttime in and of itself is not a bad thing. Without night we wouldn't have sleep, that mysterious function of our brains that renews our energy, heals our bodies, and helps us process memories, both joyful and painful. Without darkness our circadian rhythms would be interrupted, our eyes strained, our brains overworked. Think of how good it feels to simply close your eyes for a moment. Try it now. Did you find yourself taking a deep breath as you did? Light invites action and striving; darkness invites contemplation, renewal, and rest.

Then, too, there is the way an ocean or a clearing in the woods looks under the moon and the stars. We wouldn't see that beauty if it were perpetually daytime. The night itself is rarely pitch-black, but when it is, that is a kind of beauty, too. Depression is a terrible disease, and it is important that we get treatment for it as soon as possible and keep studying it so that in the future we can prevent people from suffering from it. But the darkness that often accompanies depression has gifts to offer us—if we pay attention to them.

Barbara Brown Taylor is another writer who has been a companion on the road with me. In particular, her book *Learning to Walk in the Dark* explores darkness both as a metaphor and a physical reality, and it informed my own experience during a time of spiritual darkness. She goes so far as to follow a spelunking guide into a deep, narrow cave to experience true darkness, and she observed that, "our comfort or discomfort with the outer dark is a good barometer of how we feel about the inner kind."[2]

Of spiritual darkness, Taylor writes that if she could, she would leave on night-lights to keep fear and pain from herself and her loved ones if she could only find the right night-lights to do that. But, she continues, though she fears the dark, when she finds herself in it, she doesn't find the death and terror she was expecting. "Instead," she writes, "I have learned things in the dark that I could never have learned in the light, things that have saved my life over and over again, so that there is really only one logical conclusion. I need darkness as much as I need light."[3]

Depression is brutal and evil. But times of darkness are as natural in our lives as times of light. Five hundred years ago, the Spanish mystics Saint John of the Cross and his mentor, Teresa of Avila, wrote about a deeper union with God, within the depths of our own souls. John used the imagery of a Dark Night in Spanish, *nocte oscura*, to describe how God prepares us for this union, and he writes joyfully of that night: "Oh, night that guided me, Oh night more lovely than the dawn, Oh, night that joined Beloved with lover, Lover transformed in the Beloved."[4]

Night can be a place of depth and connection with the Divine, a place of learning. The problem is when night lasts too long. Depression upsets the rhythm of night and day. That's why it used to be called the noonday demon. It was considered normal to be sad at night, but daytime sadness meant something was off. Even those of us who have not struggled with depression can relate to a long night when we are too anxious to sleep and the hours stretch out till they seem twice as long as waking hours.

Other than at the earth's poles, night and day take turns. We're sad sometimes, we're happy sometimes. Depression is a beast that traps you in a place humans weren't meant to remain. But even at the poles, night always ends. The night may be long, but it will not last forever. The day won't last forever either. The earth tilts and spins. The nature of our world is change. I think we often try to get to a place of happiness and stay there, but that isn't the reality of life. The poet Rainer Marie Rilke advises us to embrace all emotions, and understand their impermanence:

> Let everything happen to you: beauty and terror.
> Just keep going. No feeling is final.[5]

There is another reason it's important not to always describe depression as darkness. I am a white woman, living in a culture in which whiteness is consciously and subconsciously elevated and idealized. What does it mean for someone with dark skin if I speak of depression as darkness? Meri Nana-Ama Danquah addresses this in her book *Willow Weep for Me: A Black Woman's Journey through Depression*. She says, "You've heard descriptions of depression before: A black hole; an enveloping darkness; a dismal existence through which no light shines; the black dog; darkness, and more darkness. But what does darkness mean to me, a woman who has spent her life surrounded by it? The darkness of my skin; the darkness of my friends and family. I have never been afraid of the dark. It poses no harm to me."

For Meri, who has dark skin, and whose family members have dark skin, darkness has a positive connotation. To equate darkness with badness has implications for the way we value (or don't value) people with dark skin. I want to be careful, then, with how I write about darkness. Darkness may be a helpful metaphor for some of us to describe our experiences with depression, but I want to find other metaphors, too: a mental haziness that grounds you as a boat in the fog; a deep, sheer pit with no handholds to use to climb out; a debilitating sadness unrelated to life's circumstances, or related but outsized and unresponsive to the normal process of grief and recovery. I asked friends on Twitter to describe what depression feels like to them and they said: "Falling through ice, and being trapped underneath, scrabbling to find a way out," "Emptiness. A whole lot of nothing. No thoughts, energy, hope, feelings, or any way to get any of those things," "Like something very heavy is sitting on my chest," "Hopelessness. Like an invisible force pushing me under water," and "I can't breathe and my heart hurts and I'm weighed down by so much." Darkness may feel accurate sometimes, too. But I want to try not to depend too much on a metaphor that has the potential to harm people by association.

***

The inevitable cycle of lightness and darkness is mirrored by the seasons as well, as the long nights lengthen and encroach upon the day. As I'm writing this chapter it's winter again—December. The days are growing colder and, what is worse for my mood and mental health, it is darker for longer periods of time. Each afternoon brings an early and prolonged night. This is a difficult time of year for me. Tonight, sunset in Boston will be 5:33 p.m. Tomorrow, when daylight saving ends, it will be 4:32, and in a couple of weeks, it will be hit its earliest time, 4:11. The sun will set while I still have almost two hours left at work. It will set while I pick up the girl from school that I nanny. We won't return to a 5:30 sunset until the end of February. Almost four months. Four months of driving home in the dark. Four months of eating dinner with darkened windows. Darkness is descending, not just over me, not in certain places, but over the whole city, the whole country, and it feels huge and out of my control.

In these months of darkness, my rituals are important both for my body and my spirit. I light candles. I try to pause every evening when the sun sets to mark the transition—to make it feel like something I am a part of rather than something that is happening to me. I stretch out on my yoga mat, meditate and pray, breathing in the presence of the Spirit. I try to make friends with the darkness. I learn to walk in it and try to be open to its gifts and its lessons. There is no way to hurry the winter along; the only way to bring the light back is to wait. In this case, I know exactly how long I have to wait, and I mark the days. I refer to a sunset calendar every winter, marking when the sunset returns to 4:30 p.m., then to 5:00 p.m., and then to 5:45 p.m. Finally, daylight savings begins, and it is suddenly bright daylight when I get out of work, when I go to the gym in the evenings, or when I eat dinner.

Just as I had no control over the coming of the darkness, the light returns irrespective of anything I might do. Winter is long, but it will end. Your own night of depression may be short or it may be long, but it will end. I don't know what the future holds for you, but the lesson of the night and of the winter is that this time will pass. You will not always feel this way. The light is returning. And if the darkness returns again, you will have better tools to cope with it. You will have learned not to be afraid of the dark but to welcome it as a teacher and even a friend.

Notes

1. Barbara Brown Taylor, "In Praise of Darkness," *Time*, April 17, 2014, https://tinyurl.com/yywg3mde.

2. Taylor, "In Praise of Darkness."

3. Taylor, "In Praise of Darkness."

4. Saint John of the Cross, *Dark Night of the Soul* (New York: Image, 1990), 34.

5. Rainer Maria Rilke, *Rilke's Book of Hours*, trans. Anita Barrows and Joanna Macy (New York: Riverhead, 1996), 88.

10. Coping Mechanisms

You, God, who live next door—
If at times, through the long night, I trouble you
with my urgent knocking—
this is why: I hear you breathe so seldom.
I know you're all alone in that room.
If you should be thirsty, there's no one
to get you a glass of water.
I wait, listening, always. Just give me a sign!
I'm right here.
As it happens, the wall between us
is very thin. Why wouldn't a cry
from one of us
break it down? It would crumble
easily,
it would barely make a sound.

~Rainer Maria Rilke[1]

When the depression and migraines were really bad, I'd lie in bed for hours a day. Part of that was a symptom of my illnesses but part was also fulfilling a need: I was tired. Pain is exhausting, emotional pain as well as physical pain. I didn't have the kind of depression that left my mind numb. I had the kind where the pain was acute and my mind was constantly going, trying to figure out how to make it stop. I ran through my options over and over again: *Should I call a friend? Call my doctor? Change my meds myself? Go to a different therapist? Research other treatments for the migraines?*

What I really needed was a way to quiet my thoughts so my mind and spirit could rest. I was working on developing healthy ways to do that, but in the meantime, I had three less-than-perfect coping mechanisms which nevertheless worked. I binge-watched TV shows. I played computer games. And I let myself overeat: candy, ice cream, chips, whatever helped me to feel a little bit better. In an ideal world, I would have liked to be reading, meditating, and eating to nourish my body rather than to desperately numb my emotions. I was working my way toward that. But I couldn't have made it through without—at least temporarily—allowing myself those other ways to cope.

Doctor Phil used to say that you can't take away someone's unhealthy coping mechanism until you replace it with a healthy one. Healthy ones take time to learn and implement. I was doing centering prayer daily, but it had not yet helped enough to give up candy and *Grey's Anatomy*. I was getting out for walks when I could, but the migraines made it impossible to walk very far or very long, so I still spent hours a day playing *Bloons Tower Defense* on my computer.

Eventually, the healthy coping mechanisms did start to work—prayer, mediation, yoga, walking and then jogging—and I started eating more nourishing foods again and spending more time with friends and less on my computer. But it took time. If I had judged myself too harshly (or listened to those who were judging me harshly) while doing the things I needed to do to get by, it would have only led to guilt and shame, and the healing would have taken longer.

I don't know what your coping mechanisms are or what's healthy for you, or maybe less-than healthy but necessary for a time, until you're able to take better care of yourself. You are the only one that knows how hard you are trying, and what you are capable of doing. But I want to encourage you to focus on what you can do every day, even if it's only a little. Maybe you can only do fifteen minutes of yoga—that's great! Maybe you can get outside or just get out of bed and stretch, but then you need to scroll Twitter for the rest of the day to keep your mind occupied. Maybe you can cook yourself a nourishing meal once a day, but then you eat a pint of ice cream in the evening when the depression gets really bad.

There is no one path toward healing, and our various coping mechanisms are just that: ways we've learned to cope, to make it through the day. The healthier ones are, well, healthier, but they do not make you a morally better person. The person who relaxes by hiking is not more deserving of love than the person who plays video games after work.

Mary Oliver famously said, "You do not have to be good. You do not have to walk on your knees for a hundred miles through the desert repenting."[2] Not many of us would feel the necessity to do this today. But there are other things we feel we should be doing in order to be good even when they are really not required. You do not, for example, have to quit Facebook in order to be loved. You do not have to eat broccoli every day in order to be a valuable member of society. You do not have to perform in order to earn compassion from those around you. You do not have to turn off your computer and cell phone two hours before bed (although that does help you sleep). You do not have to read a Russian novel, meditate for an hour every day, or wake up before dawn to go for a run.

All you have to do is close your eyes for a minute. One minute. Just take a long, deep breath for a change. Feel the oxygen flow to your arms and feet and head. Step onto your porch and notice the sunset. Sleep in an extra ten minutes. Or maybe put some real cream in your coffee for once. Maybe the next day, close your eyes and breathe for two minutes, or five.

At the beginning of this chapter is the Rainer Marie Rilke poem to his "neighbor God" in which he wrote that the wall between them was very thin. A cry, he says, from either of them would easily break it. Why have you been doing nothing out of fear that you cannot do everything? Listen, all that stuff is lovely, good for you even, but all that is required is a word. One real word, spoken through the wall.

Or if you can't think of anything to say, just take a moment to listen. And maybe take another moment the next day, too. And even if you spend the rest of the evening binge-watching Netflix, I promise that moment will be enough to tear down the wall.

Notes

1. Rilke, *Rilke's Book of Hours*, 52.
2. Mary Oliver, *Dream Work* (New York: The Atlantic Monthly Press, 1986), 14.

11. Finding Your People (and Losing Them)

> Those who love their dream of a Christian community more than they love the Christian community itself become destroyers of that Christian community even though their personal intentions may be ever so honest, earnest and sacrificial.
>
> ~Dietrich Bonhoeffer[1]

I've been searching for community for as long as I can remember. In part, I inherited that search from my parents. We moved around so much when I was a child, and we were always looking for a church to be a part of but never quite finding a good fit. As I grew up, I was searching for something deeper than church. I was searching for fellowship, for a place where I really fit in and could be myself. I was searching for a group of people that would make me feel the way books made me feel: that we were on an adventure together, that we needed each other, that we all had gifts that complemented each other's and a role to play.

When I found the campus group at college, I tasted some of that community. I fell in love with the beautiful variety of people, all different personalities but with a common desire to know God and be real with each other. I loved that most of the other groups and cliques on campus tended to dress alike, and do their hair similarly, but in the Christian fellowship, we all did our own thing. I was drawn, also, to the LGBT group on campus even though I identified as straight and cisgender. Their signs said all were welcome, and so I went to a few of their meetings. They weren't religious meetings, but I felt the Spirit of God there as much as at the Christian fellowship.

After college, I went to an Evangelical seminary, where I never really found the community of close friends I was seeking. For my final mentored ministry, I did an internship at a large Evangelical church in Boston, living in their international student house and filling various ministry roles. It was a great experience but living in a dorm setting and sharing a kitchen with nine other people convinced me that I needed more personal space. I decided to look for my own apartment or one with just one other housemate.

Instead, for financial reasons as well as the fear of loneliness and the deep, sheer pit of depression, I responded to an ad for an intentional Christian community. The people were warm and friendly, the food homemade, the children adorable, and the house much lovelier than anything I'd be able to afford otherwise. At age thirty-two, having just sworn off communal living, I moved into an even bigger community than I'd ever lived in before. A year later, the worst depressive episode of my life began, and for better or for worse, over the next several years this community was where it was going to play out.

Even though I craved solitude, I ran toward community. Maybe I wouldn't have experienced such a devastating depression if I'd allowed myself the quiet and the time alone I needed. On the other hand, I think I'd been pushing off the depression for so long it was bound to hit me eventually. And as hard as things were in the community at times, I think it was better to go through the depression there than living on my own. Henri Nouwen had a similar experience when he went through a breakdown shortly after moving into the community L'Arche in Toronto:

> The strange thing was that this happened shortly after I had found my true home. After many years of life in universities, where I never felt fully at home, I had become a member of L'Arche, a community of men and women with mental disabilities. I had been received with open arms, given all the attention and affection I could ever hope for, and offered a safe and loving place to grow spiritually as well as emotionally. Everything seemed ideal. But precisely at that time I fell apart—as if I needed a safe place to hit bottom.[2]

My friends in the house offered me a safe place in some ways, especially Matteo, who struggled with his own mental health challenges and was empathetic and caring in a way I'd never experienced before. My other housemates and I found a lot of common ground in our dream of community and our appreciation of music, art, and deep conversations. We participated in evening prayers together each night and sitting in the cozy front room singing and praying with them was the closest I'd ever felt to my dream of community.

It wasn't long, though, before cracks began to appear in that dream. My own worsening depression became an object of disagreement in our house. Other than Matteo, my housemates couldn't understand why I was changing before their eyes. They had seen a cheerful, productive Jessica when I first moved into the community, and they thought I should be able to get myself back to that place again. We tried to talk and understand each other's perspectives, but it became too hard for me to stay there, and I ended up moving to another house in the community. Those friendships, which were so important to me, were fractured and never fully healed.

After that, I began to lean even more heavily on Matteo, and he tried to put some distance between us for the sake of his own health. Another friend in the community set similar boundaries. I was devastated and began to feel like I was losing all my friends and especially the one who was most able to help me when the depression was bad

There is a quote that I see shared often online, variously attributed to Glennon Doyle, Karen Salmansohn, and others: "You will be too much for some people. Those are not your people." I think it's true that some people can't truly accept us for who we are, and so it's time for us to move on. But I actually think some of the people we're too much for may be our people, they just can't be our only people. We need a team. We can go to some people for a certain kind of support, and others for another. Or we can split the support we need—as well as the support we can offer—between more than one person.

As young Marcus noted when his mother was suffering from depression in the movie *About A Boy*:

> Suddenly I realized: two people weren't enough. You need backup. If there are only two people, and someone drops off the edge, then you're on your own. Two isn't a large enough number. You need three at least.[3]

Or, as the Bible puts it, "A cord of three strands is not quickly broken."[4]

Depression complicates this, though, for several reasons. You can't always think clearly enough to articulate your needs or sort out what you need from whom. And of course, you don't really know what you need, especially at first. You don't know what people can do that would help, you just wish somebody would do something.

Sometimes even when you're able to identify and name what you need, the people around you are not able to offer it to you. And when you're knocked out, exhausted from fighting the beast of depression every moment of every day, it's often impossible to even take a shower, much less go out and find new friends to support you. Sometimes, too, your people are trying to tell you what they can offer, but all you can hear is rejection. They may be simply telling you their own needs and boundaries, but what you hear is that you are too much for them, and probably for anyone. Depression is isolating in so many ways.

Henri Nouwen wrote a lot about his own feelings of loneliness and rejection, particularly when a close friend had had to set boundaries with him. He wrote to himself,

> You keep listening to those who seem to reject you. But they never speak about *you*. They speak about their own limitations. They confess their poverty in the face of your needs and desires. They simply ask for your compassion. They do not say that you are bad, ugly, or despicable. They say only that you are asking for something they cannot give and that they need to get some distance from you to survive emotionally. The sadness is that you perceive their necessary withdrawal as a rejection of you instead of as a call to return home and discover there your true belovedness.[5]

As I've recovered from major depression and rebuilt my support system, I've begun thinking of my various friends and family as lifelines. In a popular TV game show, *Who Wants to Be a Millionaire*, contestants must answer questions of increasing difficulty to earn increasingly more money. If they do not know the answer, or do not feel confident in their response, they can use one of their three lifelines: Ask the audience, 50:50, or phone a friend. Each lifeline has different strategic benefits, and since they can only use each one once, they must decide which question best fits with each lifeline.[6]

I often think of my various friends and communities in this way. I don't have one friend that I can go to with every emotion, question, desire, or need—I don't think it is even healthy to ask another person to bear that much for me. But I know I can vent about chronic illness to Matteo and he will understand, or text Gina and she will immediately pray for me. I can message Susi and she will be ready to offer her limited free time for a lunch date, or I can express my frustrations about misogyny to Laura or Fen, and they will respond with empathy and readiness to fight on my behalf. In other words, I've built a team. And knowing I have these lifelines helps me also to know when I actually don't need them—when I am strong enough to take a deep breath and press on by myself.

Depression makes you feel alone, and rejection, or felt-rejection, from friends, can intensify this feeling. But maybe you have more friends than you realize; you have just been asking the wrong people for the wrong things. Write a list of the people who are potential lifelines and what they have offered in support. Maybe even write a list of your own needs and talk to your friends about what they can offer. Someone who would be overwhelmed by a phone call at three in the morning may be happy and grateful to respond to a daytime text for prayer or to swing by with a bag of groceries. Another person may feel overwhelmed at the thought of buying groceries but goes to bed late anyway and would be glad to talk. And for another person, just knowing you are there and understand what they're going through might make *you* a vital part of *their* team.

Notes

1. Dietrich Bonhoeffer, *Life Together: A Discussion of Christian Fellowship* (New York: Harper & Row, 1954), 27.

2. Nouwen, *Inner Voice of Love*, xiii–xiv.

3. Chris Weitz, Paul Weitz, and Peter Hedges, *About a Boy*, DVD, directed by Chris Weitz and Paul Weitz (Universal City: Universal Pictures, 2002).

4. Eccles 4:9–12.

5. Nouwen, *Inner Voice of Love*, 13.

6. I am remembering an older version of the game. The lifelines have since changed somewhat.

12. Finding Your People Online

Those days I laid in bed, barely leaving my room, I did more on my computer than watching Netflix and playing games. I got on Facebook, as well (Twitter would come later). I added everyone I could think of as friends, and I scrolled their posts, sometimes out of loneliness or jealousy, sometimes just out of curiosity about what everyone else was doing, and how they were going about living their lives. After a while, I began to find online communities that gathered around shared interests or passions. I was too exhausted to leave my room, but I began making friends online, joining in discussions, adding my own thoughts to posts. These communities would become vital to my own connection with the world.

One of the first communities I found was a small group called Momastery, a group composed of mostly women, run by Glennon Doyle. They called themselves Monkees back then, and there were only a thousand or so of them. I got to know Glennon and through her, other women who would become good friends—Aimee, Neile, Arwen, Dawn, Anna, Beth, and many others. When Glennon's blog posts began to go viral, her followers grew to the ten-thousands and then hundred-thousands. But though the group has lost its original intimacy, there is still something special about the Momastery community and those who post there. When I found Momastery, the depression was a bit better, but it was still hard for me to do much outside of the house, and having online connections and conversations with the women there helped me to feel connected to the world. Glennon set the tone by telling us to, "Be brave because you are a child of God. Be kind because everyone else is, too."[1]

Another amazing online community I'm a part of was created by Jenny Lawson, who goes by the blogging name The Bloggess. Lawson struggles with depression and other mental health issues, and many folks have found in her, and each other, the freedom to share their struggles honestly. At one point a few years ago, Lawson started a thread on her blog for people who wanted to connect on Twitter, and I joined a few hundred members of what we would call The Bloggess Tribe. I deeply appreciate the honesty and openness of the members of The Bloggess Tribe. The group embodies the idea of "come as you are," and I know many have found friends and community there. Here's what Jenny wrote one night, reaching out to her many followers so that we—and she—would feel less alone:

> I'm having one of those nights where – against all logic – I find myself feeling small. Not a good small, like "Aren't you adorable? I want to put you in my pocket" but that insignificant, unimportant sort of small. The kind that makes you feel like you're just dust that could spin out into space, or that the night is so dark that you'll never be found or remembered. The kind that

makes every personal failing magnified to the point it's physically painful. I don't know where these nights come from, but I suspect they come to us all . . . making us doubt that we exist, that we matter, that we will ever get our shit together.

Maybe some people don't have nights like these. Maybe I just say to myself that it's normal because if it's not then that niggling sense of failure and fear that floods over me is based on reality. I know it's not. Logically, I know it, but logic doesn't work well on nights like this. I go through my mind and count the facts and try to discount the fear and panic. I fail. I am small. But I also succeed sometimes too. I am important. I am insignificant. I am a speck of dust. I am necessary. They're all true.

But on nights like these I push back in the dark and tell myself that tomorrow the sun will shine and this night will be past. I will have beaten the darkness that seeps into my heart when things shift, and rifts appear. I will have beaten it simply by existing long enough to find the sun again.

I am small. But if that's true then so, too, are my fears and doubts. They seem so large, but they live in me so they can't be bigger than I am. I will win. By sheer volume. And I'll keep repeating that to myself until I finally believe it, or until the morning comes. Whichever comes first.[2]

Jenny's honesty in sharing about her struggles ennobles others to share about theirs as well. It is powerful to have someone boldly say the very thing we've been ashamed of for so long. It is her vulnerability as much as her words of hope that encourage me and so many others.

Bunmi Laditan is another writer who has been a companion on the way for me, and who has built her Facebook page into a community. She is open about her struggles with depression and motherhood in general, and she creates space for others to be open as well. Her particular focus is on motherhood, and she addresses postpartum depression in her writing and tweets as well as depression in general:

> One of the major characters in *Confessions of a Domestic Failure II* has crippling postpartum depression. Writing her character is filling me with empathy for myself and all of the woman who have walked this dark road. It's not you, babe. There's no shame in getting help.[3]

> When you have anxiety/depression, it's important to remember you don't deserve every feeling that comes along.[4]

> Suicide isn't as simple as being happy or sad, it's about being sick. Depression isn't a mood or emotion, it is an illness.[5]

Someone else who is similarly creating community on social media is writer Jonny Sun. Jonny is open about his depression and anxiety in a way that gives glimpses of hope while still acknowledging how hard it is.

I know this is an entry-level message but we have to destigmatize it. i didnt grow up having language to acknowledge mental health, and when i finally learned it, the world opened. depression is a lonely monster but depression, unacknowledged and unseen, is infinitely lonelier.[6]

Every time i tweet about my anxiety or depression, so many people respond and relate and honestly it's so assuring and helpful. it makes it so these experiences dont feel so isolating lonely. i'm so grateful for all of you.[7]

A quote from an article about Jonny Sun in the *New York Times* gives insight into the role people like Glennon Doyle, Jenny Lawson, Bunmi Laditan, and Jonny Sun play on social media:

Not long ago, Sun was invited to the wedding of two people he had never met. The couple had found each other online through their shared loved of jomny son tweets. As Sun sees it, social-media platforms are like urban landscapes, in which popular accounts function almost like landmarks. They are spaces where people go to interact and encounter one another; people imbue them with meaning and, over time, a shared history.[8]

Social media helps us find people. We begin by following a person who is speaking of things we can relate to—in these cases depression and loneliness, among other things—and then through those people, we meet others who relate, and we discover that we are not nearly as alone as we thought we were.

Other social media platforms start out with the intent of gathering people for community and discussion. Slate Speak is a Thursday evening Progressive Christian discussion group originally created by Jason Chesnut (@crazypastor on Twitter) under the auspices of The Slate Project. A diverse range of people take turns moderating. They tackle subjects like racial justice and the Bible. Every Thursday night at 9PM Eastern time they start by asking everyone to introduce themselves, give their preferred pronouns, and answer an ice breaker question. Then there is a prayer followed by this note: "We're not automatically agreeing with everything that we/the moderator says. #SlateSpeak is a safe space for questions, critiques, and challenges. You can follow along silently but feel free to engage if/when you feel comfortable."[9]

It is one of the kindest, most open places on the internet, while at the same time relentlessly exploring themes of justice and how they relate to the church. As their website explains it: "A big part of our project is 'self-critique' of our church institutions, theologies, and practices. We know there is a lot that needs to be 'cleaned off the slate'—like all the ways racism, sexism, homophobia, classism, xenophobia, colonialism, patriarchy, disrespect for other religions, and a bunch of other bad stuff—have been a part of the structures of the church and the way we relate to one another."[10] Even though I'm often asleep before it's over, I have really appreciated their conversations, and have made some lasting connections by participating.

Then there are the hashtag movements through which I've found friends who share some of my experiences and perspectives. #Exvangelical is a group of people who were immersed in the Evangelical church or other Evangelical communities and have left. Some are still Christians, others are not, but they share a common past and many carry trauma from their experiences and are helping each other learn how to process and heal. #Churchtoo is a hashtag started by Emily Joy and Hannah Paasch, inspired by the #metoo movement, to discuss sexual abuse and assault in Christian contexts. #Milleneagram is a hashtag started by Hannah Paasch to discuss the way the Enneagram can teach us about ourselves and help us grow and heal. #Faithfullylgbt was started by Eliel Cruz for LGBTQIA people of faith to connect and share their perspectives.

On Facebook there are groups like Raising Children Unfundamentalist, started by writer Cindy Wang Brandt, and Contemplative Writers run by Ed Cyzewski, Andi Cumbo-Floyd, Tara Owens, and Emily Miller. Another way to meet people online is to join a book launch team for a writer you like. Many teams continue chatting long after the book has been launched.

Often online communities and friendships are criticized for not being real, but these friendships have been very real to me and have helped me during times when I could not make it out of the house for in-person gatherings. Even now, when I do make it out more often, I keep going online to connect with people and communities there. I know this is true for many other folks as well. The communities I've mentioned may not be for you, but there are resources out there that may fit your needs and interests. There are friendships and connections to be made, and many people who know what you are going through because they're going through it, too.

If you'd like to explore social media landmarks and communities, but aren't interested in any of the ones I've listed, try searching your interests with hashtags on Twitter or Instagram. Take your interest and put a pound sign in front of it: #anxiety #depression #model-trains #modernart #philosphy #CSLewis, etc. Or, alternately, look for landmarks, for people who are well-known in that field, and pay attention to the discussion happening under their posts. Leave a comment. Tell something true about yourself, and see who writes back, "Me, too!"

Notes

1. Glennon Doyle, "Glennon speaking at Old South Church in Boston," *Instagram*, July 1, 2015, https://tinyurl.com/y3hc6xvw.

2. Jenny Lawson, "One of Those Nights," *The Bloggess*, August 7, 2016, https://tinyurl.com/y29ak28z.

3. Bunmi Laditan, Twitter post, November 13, 2017, 4:36 p.m., https://tinyurl.com/y2utr2sf.

4. Bunmi Laditan, Twitter post, August 15, 2018, 2:12 p.m., https://tinyurl.com/y2h4bgmt.

5. Bunmi Laditan, Twitter post, June 5, 2018, 11:58 a.m.,

https://tinyurl.com/yxoutgw2.

6. Jonny Sun, Twitter post, June 8, 2018, 10:16 a.m., https://tinyurl.com/yyvt75k8.

7. Jonny Sun, Twitter post, November 3, 2018, 3:09 a.m., https://tinyurl.com/y2wx2cun.

8. Jesse Lichtenstein, "A Whimisical Wordsmith Charts a Course Beyond Twitter," *New York Times*, June 15, 2017, https://tinyurl.com/y8mhab2p.

9. Rachel Damayanthi, Twitter post, May 9, 2019, 8:12 p.m., https://tinyurl.com/y3lm345b.

10. "Who We Are," *Slate Project*, https://tinyurl.com/yyg62p3g.

13. Finding Your True Calling

Your unique presence in your community is the way God wants you to be present to others. Different people have different ways of being present. You have to know and claim your way. That is why discernment is so important. Once you have an inner knowledge of your true vocation, you have a point of orientation. That will help you decide what to do and what to let go of, what to say and what to remain silent about, when to go out and when to stay home, who to be with and who to avoid. When you get exhausted, frustrated, overwhelmed, or run down, your body is saying that you are doing things that are none of your business. God does not require of you what is beyond your ability, what leads you away from God, or what makes you depressed or sad. God wants you to live for others and to live that presence well. . . . You have not yet fully found your place in your community. Your way of being present to your community may require times of absence, prayer, writing, or solitude. These too are times for your community.

~Henri Nouwen[1]

My thirties turned out to be a time of leaving. First, I left my ministry job and along with it, regular church attendance since my church was intricately connected to my ministry job. Finally, a few months before my fortieth birthday, I left the community where I had lived for seven years. There were many good things in my decade of immersion in church, ministry, and community. But there were some really hard things as well, and I came away with symptoms of trauma and a lot of difficult experiences that I needed to work through. For so long, I'd been trying to work and heal within the structure of a religious community. But each act of leaving, though painful and traumatic, freed me in profound ways that allowed me to understand my true self, my relationship with God, and to pursue my true calling. It was not until I left the community that I began writing regularly, even though writing has been my dream since I was young. It was not until I had my own quiet living room and porch (shared with just one quite housemate) that I could sit on my couch or lie on my yoga mat and breathe in deep draughts of healing.

I stayed in the community for so long because I was afraid to be alone. But once I left, I was amazed at how quickly the healing came. It's hard to heal from trauma when you are in the situation that caused the trauma. It's hard to listen to the insistent but often quiet voice of God's leading in your life when you are surrounded by other people's expectations of you (and yours of them). And it's hard to acknowledge the ways you've changed when you're around people who have not changed in the same way.

I still believe in the power of community and particularly spiritual community. As the author of Hebrews says, "[do not give] up meeting together, as some are in the habit of doing."[2] I still believe we need each other to nourish our faith. Not just the hand-picked friends who are like us and support us, but the whole body of Christ, broken and difficult. This includes those who speak different languages than we do, literally and figuratively, those who are in different places than we are, those who we can learn from and those who can learn from us. But we can't offer our gifts and ourselves, and we can't learn from others unless we are caring for ourselves first.

It was during my hours of solitude that I wrote essays that spoke to others and helped them feel less alone. It was out of the quiet that I found the right words to speak about God in ways that helped others feel God's presence. It was my "creative absence" from structured community that gave me the freedom to grow into my true calling and to find friends who shared and supported that calling.

Your story is different than mine, of course. For one thing, you may be more of an extrovert, needing interaction in order to feel energized and inspired. Your calling is different than mine because you are different. You are unique, and because of this, you have something unique to offer others. As much as you need other people, they need you too. Not you pretending to be something that you're not, but *you*. The *you* who is leaning in to your true vocation, the Latin word for calling, which you sense in your deepest being when you are quiet and alone with God. This vocation is not necessarily a career or a specific field. It is you being fully you and bringing that full self to others.

The question of vocation is given quite a bit of attention in today's society with so many more options for careers and volunteering than there were a hundred or even fifty years ago (though I can't write that sentence without acknowledging that there are many more choices for those with the privilege of generational financial stability and connections, a privilege that, in America, exits disproportionately among white people). I first took an aptitude test in eighth grade; I don't remember the results, but I remember that for some reason, I was very scared of learning that I was supposed to be a social worker, so I carefully answered no to all of the questions about enjoying serving others. (I did end up being a social worker for a couple of years in my late twenties.) Some people find their calling, or at least their field of work, fairly early on and settle into it for most of their lives. But there are many of us who read books and take tests and try different things, spending considerable amounts of time uncertain of where our gifts and dreams are pointing us.

Frederick Buechner's suggested way of finding our calling is to look for the place where, "your deep gladness and the world's deep hunger meet." As he explains,

> There are all different kinds of voices calling you to all different kinds of work, and the problem is to find out which is the voice of God rather than of Society, say, or the Super-ego, or Self-Interest.
> By and large a good rule for finding out is this.

The kind of work God usually calls you to is the kind of work (a) that you need most to do and (b) that the world most needs to have done. If you really get a kick out of your work, you've presumably met requirement (a), but if your work is writing TV deodorant commercials, the chances are you've missed requirement (b). On the other hand, if your work is being a doctor in a leper colony, you have probably met requirement (b), but if most of the time you're bored and depressed by it, the chances are you have not only bypassed (a) but probably aren't helping your patients much either.

Neither the hair shirt nor the soft berth will do. The place God calls you to is the place where your deep gladness and the world's deep hunger meet.[3]

I like Buechner's definition though I would say that there are deodorant commercial writers who are also living out their calling. I think if it's where you're supposed to be, it's possible to find joy in it *and* find ways to serve others in it. Sometimes, too, a job is just a job, and our real calling is how we spend the hours when we aren't working, or how we spend the moments of interaction with our coworkers and clients.

Glennon Doyle offers a similar suggestion to Buechner, but instead of looking for our deep gladness, she suggests looking at our heartbreak:

Pain knocks on everyone's door. If we are wise, we will greet it and say, Come in, sit down, and don't leave until you've taught me what I need to know. Allow heartbreak to guide you at every turn. Ask yourself: What breaks your heart? At least once a day, I hear some version of this: "Oh, I can't bear to look at that rescue dog. It breaks my heart." "I can't read about those poor Syrian refugees." "I can't visit my friend in the oncology ward. It's too hard seeing her that way." As if our hearts were meant to be returned to our maker in pristine condition! No, the heart is like any other muscle: It has to be worked, even ripped apart in order to grow stronger. We must get familiar with heartbreak, become curious about it, because there we will find essential clues for solving the mystery of who we are intended to be.[4]

Times of depression or other struggles may obscure our gladness, but they do have a way of showing us clearly what breaks our heart. Those times also have a way of showing us the areas where we were faking gladness, because when you are depressed, it becomes impossible to fake it any more. For me, depression stripped away my ability to continue working for an Evangelical ministry. It was devastating, but it ultimately brought me the freedom to choose a path that was better for me. Could it maybe be offering a similarly difficult gift to you?

Another thing about calling is that as we grow, we change, hopefully more and more into who we are truly meant to be. And as we change, what we are doing with our lives may change as well. It's not failure to admit that the job we've worked at for a time is no longer the right fit for us. As Michelle Obama wrote, "Now I think it's one of the most useless questions an adult can ask a child—What do you want to be when you grow up? As if growing up is finite. As if at some point you become something and that's the end."[5]

Ivy Anthony also focuses on the idea of calling as a changeable thing in her sermon on life as improvisation, with God as your improv partner. She talks about the role of nurse-maid that Miriam leapt into when Pharaoh's daughter found Miriam's baby brother, Moses, hidden in the reeds of the Nile River:

> To improvise in life requires great listening to others and the spirit of God. This listening allows us to create new ways forward—paths unseen. I can imagine that Miriam's first steps into the Nile River were taken from listening to God, where God nudged her "go, Miriam, go" and all of the steps to follow, unknown and unpredictable, were bolstered by this knowing of God's steady voice. It allows her to work within the limitations of her reality as a slave, and yet utilize a social structure that she knows where royalty, upon seeing a baby, would need a nurse-maid.
>
> Our life with God is a life where we are welcomed into a story that is continually being created in the moment with players and actors that we have never met. And yet the call, that I think Miriam responds to and that we are all invited to, is to say "yes" to all of that before the plans are laid out and to take what we do know of ourselves and God with courage to the scene,

and trust that that is enough to create some-thing we can't predict.[6]

Whether you have a sense of your current calling or not, whether you are working in a field that brings you gladness and meets the world's need or sweating through every hour of a job you hate or lying in bed, unable to work because of your health—we need you. The Bible uses the metaphor of a body to describe the church and says that even the weak are indispensable. Not that the weak are tolerated or carried out of char-ity or pity but that they are indispensable. Even if, right now, you can't get out of bed for more than half an hour a day, you are part of us. We need you.

> The eye cannot say to the hand, "I don't need you!" And the head cannot say to the feet, "I don't need you!" On the contrary, those parts of the body that seem to be weaker are indispens-able, and the parts that we think are less honor-able we treat with special honor. And the parts that are unpresentable are treated with special modesty, while our presentable parts need no special treatment. But God has put the body together, giving greater honor to the parts that lacked it, so that there should be no division in the body, but that its parts should have equal concern for each other. If one part suffers, every part suffers with it; if one part is honored, every part rejoices with it.[7]

We all need each other in order to function well and fully, as a compassionate, intelligent, productive body.

If even one of us is missing, we aren't complete. As Frederick Buechner wrote:

> The grace of God means something like: Here is your life. You might never have been, but you are because the party wouldn't have been complete without you. Here is the world. Beautiful and terrible things will happen. Don't be afraid. I am with you. Nothing can ever separate us. It's for you I created the universe. I love you. There's only one catch. Like any other gift, the gift of grace can be yours only if you'll reach out and take it. Maybe being able to reach out and take it is a gift too.[8]

Welcome to the party, friend. We've missed you, and we're glad you're here. Come in and sit at the table with the rest of us who are weak yet indispensable.

Notes

1. Nouwen, *Inner Voice of Love*, 68.
2. Hebrews 10:25.
3. Frederick Buechner, *Wishful Thinking*, 118–19.
4. Glennon Doyle Melton, "The Important Lesson You Can Learn from Heartbreak," Oprah, https://tinyurl.com/y4woxwfq.
5. Michelle Obama, *Becoming* (New York: Crown, 2018), ix.
6. Ivy Anthony, "The Steadiness of Improvising," *Reservoir Church*, June 9, 2019, https://tinyurl.com/y3jop7tq.

7. 1 Cor 12:21–26.

8. Frederick Buechner, *Wishful Thinking: A Seeker's ABC* (New York: Harper One, 1973), 39.

14. Depression Lies

You may have heard people say that depression lies. It tells you things about yourself and your situation that are not true. It's not just that you are focusing on the negative and forgetting to think about the good things in life. It is as if the good things have ceased to exist. It is as if you were listening to a full orchestra and then, suddenly or one by one, all the instruments began to drop out except for the bass. You know in theory that the music is playing—that the sun is shining, that you have family and friends who love you, that every life has value including yours—but all you can hear is that deep, low note. In the same way, your inner messages which, in depression's absence, vary throughout the day and week—*that was fun; I'm nervous; I look kind of cute in this jacket; that baby's laugh is contagious; I hope my mom's surgery goes well; I'm tired; I'm hungry; I love her*—fade away to the dull grey messages of depression—*I'm worthless. Nobody loves me. I'll never accomplish anything.* A deep, low note of hopelessness.

Depression not only lies, it lies really, really well. It knows your weak points with surgical precision. It knows which lies are most likely to ring true to you because these lies go along with your deep sense of an inner flaw, which has been there since you were a child. There are common themes to these lies, but each person's fears and insecurities are sharply specific to

them. Often our friends will try to reach us with affir-
mations that have helped them, but since they're not
responding to our own specific inner messages, they're
not helpful. It's so important to know what these exact
lies are for each of us so that we will recognize them
when they are spoken by the depression or by other
people.

One tool that has been really helpful to me in dis-
cerning my specific fears is the Enneagram. The
Enneagram breaks down the basic personalities into
nine types, which are each predisposed to receive a
different message about the world and themselves. In
their book *The Wisdom of the Enneagram*, Don
Richard Riso and Russ Hudson describe the uncon-
scious messages that each type received as a child. You
don't have to be familiar with the Enneagram or what
the types refer to, but a quick glance at the list below
will reveal that there are nine basic messages that children internalize.

Type One: It's not ok to make mistakes.

Type Two: It's not ok to have your own needs.

Type Three: It's not ok to have your own feelings
and identity.

Type Four: It's not ok to be too functional or too
happy.

Type Five: It's not ok to be comfortable in the
world.

Type Six: It's not ok to trust yourself.

Type Seven: It's not ok to depend on anyone for anything.

Type Eight: It's not ok to be vulnerable or to trust anyone.

Type Nine: It's not ok to assert yourself.[1]

So, some of us may have received the message, whether from our parents, our caregivers, or our culture in general, that it's not okay to make mistakes. Because of that, every mistake we made in childhood felt like a terrible failure; we tried to be perfect but could never quite obtain that perfection. Others of us may have somehow heard the message that it's not okay to have feelings, and so we pushed those feelings down, but no matter how hard we tried, our feelings always found a way to surface. They still do. Those childhood messages, and the subsequent ways we believe we fall short, haunt everyone to some degree. But when depression comes, it adds fuel to the fire. We start to believe that we have a fatal flaw, a lie we believe about ourselves that we think will be our downfall.

Here's my own attempt to rewrite Riso and Hudson's childhood messages into the language of fatal flaws. The truth is that these aren't fatal, and they are not necessarily even flaws, but rather, they point us to the way we can grow through vulnerability and understanding. Try to read each one slowly and think about how it makes you feel. Is it something you believe about the world or yourself in particular? Do you think there might be a deeper truth about yourself that your upbringing or the depression is masking?

You may fear:

> That your fatal flaw is that you make mistakes; that you aren't perfect.
>
> That your fatal flaw is that you are too needy; you secretly care about yourself more than others.
>
> That your fatal flaw is that you have your own feelings and personality that don't go along with society's expectations.
>
> That your fatal flaw is that you are different than everyone else, and you will never belong or be happy.
>
> That your fatal flaw is that you need the comforts of this world, including relationships with other people.
>
> That your fatal flaw is that deep down you believe your instincts rather than others' opinions.
>
> That your fatal flaw is that you need other people, and they can see your need.
>
> That your fatal flaw is that you have deep weaknesses and vulnerabilities that others may be able to exploit.
>
> That your fatal flaw is that you have a strong personality and strong opinions that may overwhelm others.

If none of these fatal flaws rings true to you, don't worry. This is just one tool. Talk to your therapist about it, journal about it; see if you can articulate the very specific lies that depression is telling you. Then you will be better able to counter them with very specific truths.

In addition to the childhood messages we receive, there are also lost childhood messages. These are the truths that we needed to hear as children but didn't, or we didn't hear them clearly enough that they stuck. Each of us feels the lack of a particular message the most, but together all nine are important to know and believe about ourselves. Try reading them to yourself as if you are your own parent, telling your inner child the real truths about herself to combat the lies.

> You are good.
> You are wanted.
> You are loved for yourself.
> You are seen for who you are.
> Your needs are not a problem.
> You are safe.
> You will be taken care of.
> You will not be betrayed.
> Your presence matters.[2]

No matter what type you are, each of these nine statements is true about you. You are good because God looked on God's creation and called it good. You are wanted because the one who created the universe in all its beauty and complexity felt that your existence was important, and created you, too. You are loved for yourself, by God and others, and don't have to earn that love. You are seen for who you are, by your creator and by those close to you, and you can express that true self creatively to help others feel less alone. Your needs are not a problem—you are hungry because it is good to eat, you need love and friendship because those are good things to need and to pursue. You are safe, despite the uncertainty of the world, and you can live fully in the moment without fear of what is to come because the moment is all that really exists. You will be taken care of; there are people who care and will care for you when you need help. You will not be betrayed; there are those worthy of your trust. Your presence matters. We need you here.

If you can't believe these truths today, hold on. Keep repeating them to yourself, replacing the lies with the true messages, and slowly, over time, the truth will become stronger. The flutes, cellos, trumpets and timpani will return to the orchestra's swell. Your own voice will return, and it will be surer and more confident than before. The world waits anxiously for you and loves you for who you are now, who you were, and who you will be.

Notes

1. Don Richard Riso and Russ Hudson, *The Wisdom of the Enneagram: The Complete Guide to Psychological and Spiritual Growth for the Nine Personality Types* (New York: Bantam, 1999), 31.

2. Riso and Hudson, *Wisdom of the Enneagram*, 34.

15. My Own Fatal Flaw

*A note for readers: In this chapter I talk about body image and disordered eating, which may be a trigger for some people.

It is, finally, so wonderful to have learned to eat, to taste and love what slips down my throat, padding me, fill me up, that I'm not uncomfortable calling it a small miracle. A friend who does not believe in God says, "Maybe not a miracle, but a little improvement," but to that I say, Listen! You must not have heard me right; I couldn't feed myself! So thanks for your input, but I know where I was, and I know where I am now, and you just can't get here from there. Something happened that I had despaired would ever happen. It was like being a woman who has despaired of ever getting to be a mother but who now cradles a baby. So it was either a miracle—Picasso said, "Everything is a miracle; it's a miracle that one does not dissolve in one's bath like a lump of sugar"—or maybe it was more of a gift, one that required some assembly. But whatever it was, learning to eat was about learning to live—and deciding to live;

and it is one of the most radical things I've ever done.

~Anne Lamott[1]

For most of my life, I thought my weight was my fatal flaw. From early childhood I'd gleaned from my parents, my peers, and the persistent commercial culture I was steeped in that I was getting too big, and unless I could somehow get smaller, I was never going to be truly loved or happy. But I was too hungry to eat less and too tired to exercise more (a fatigue I now attribute to the beginnings of chronic migraines), and besides, food was a comfort, both physically and mentally. I would try to limit my eating, but then the subsequent intensifying hunger would make me eat even more than I probably would have originally. And so, beyond my weight, I began to feel I had a fatal flaw of stubbornness that made me refuse to do what I needed to lose weight and that this stubbornness was going to prevent me from ever being loved or happy.

I felt that these flaws were confirmed, in many small ways, throughout elementary school and middle school, and then in larger ways in high school and college when I started dating and received only conditional love and affirmation from my boyfriends. I was beautiful, fierce, intelligent, and even wise for my age, and part of me knew the flaw was on their end, not on mine. Yet, the sense of my own deep, inner flaw was difficult to ignore. I learned ways to starve myself and to push myself in exercise despite the fact that it would trigger migraines. I lost weight, gained it back, lost more, and gained back more. In my senior year in college, I delved deeper into starvation, limiting myself to five hundred calories some days. My boyfriend approved of my diminishing figure. It was intoxicating. And then the depression came swooping in.

When I graduated from college and broke up with that boyfriend, I gained back the weight that I had lost, plus another forty pounds. I'd starved my body—could I blame it for desperately trying to live? But now I found myself in my mid-twenties, bigger than I'd ever been. It was almost a self-fulfilling prophecy. If my fatal flaw was my weight, then there it was, obvious to me and everyone else. I tried to eat well and exercise, and even though I managed to lose a few pounds, most of the weight was still there when I moved into the community at age thirty-two.

There I found myself losing weight in what seemed to be a healthy way, eating sufficient portions of healthy food and going for long, relaxing walks. But just when the weight came off, the depression got really bad. I felt strongly that there was a connection between the two. If my fatal flaw was my weight, and I was losing weight in a healthy way this time, why was this triggering a deep depression? Shouldn't I be happy?

As I learned to be quiet and listen to God through centering prayer, I also learned to listen to my body. What I found was that, at a very early age, I'd identified eating when I was hungry as a flaw. I would eat a regular meal and still be hungry, but I got the message from the adults around me that having seconds, or an after-dinner snack, represented a lack of discipline. It wasn't that my parents withheld food from me, but I could tell that they themselves felt they'd failed when they ate extra snacks and helpings. I remember once asking my dad if it was more polite at my friend's house to take a large first portion or to take a small one then ask for seconds. He responded that the best thing wasn't to take much at all. I wish I could go back and tell both of us that most hosts are happy when their cooking is appreciated!

What I've come to realize is that I was receiving the message that my basic instincts were wrong. To eat when you are hungry is necessary for survival. To internalize the message that my own sense of hunger was not reliable, damaged my sense of trust in my own intuition and self-knowledge. That damaged trust affected not just my eating but every aspect of my life, physical, emotional, and spiritual.

My instinct, my desire for food and for survival, was what I'd labeled stubbornness, and I worked as hard as I could to fight against it. That stubbornness, that refusal to accept the world's judgement of me was the spark of life at the core of my existence. To give it up was to die, to starve to death emotionally, just as giving up eating when I was hungry was to die physically. But to hold on to it felt like destining myself to never find human love or acceptance.

This insight helped me to see how I'd internalized the same message about the migraines and depression that I had about my weight: *"This is my fault. Why am I so stubborn?"* It was a hard message to counteract. As anyone with a chronic illness knows, 99 percent of your daily energy goes into micromanaging your health. With my migraines in particular, there are so many triggers to be avoided at every turn—sunlight, fluorescent lights, flashing lights (the slow crawl of traffic past the flashing police cars and ambulance lights of an accident can take me out for days), motion sickness, heat, humidity, lack of sleep, too much sleep, exercise, not getting enough exercise, over-medication, under-medication, shoulder tension, not enough water, going too long without eating, too much salt, MSG, caffeine or not enough caffeine, too much social interaction, standing up too fast—the list is almost endless. So, whenever I got a migraine, it was easy to point to something on that list and blame myself.

Likewise, with depression, there are things you can do to reduce depression and lower the risk of having another major depressive episode. But all those things—exercise, getting outside, keeping in touch with friends, meditating, eating healthy foods, taking your meds, etc.—are harder when you are actually depressed. And when you combine two or more chronic illnesses, the number of daily decisions you have to make that will affect your health are almost infinite. To a degree, this kind of scrutiny is helpful for developing routines and a lifestyle that minimizes the pain. But the constant self-analysis is exhausting and leads to a constant sense of guilt. I did twenty things today to treat and prevent the migraines and depression. Should I have done twenty-five?

I noticed a spiritual connection to this guilt and self-examination, too. In many of the churches I've attended, there is a weekly confession of sins in which we pray: "Forgive me for what I have done and for what

I have left undone." Every week that prayer is said, and even as a child I remember struggling with the implications. We were supposed to try as hard as we could to not sin, but even as we tried, the church secretary was printing up the bulletin with that confession in it for next Sunday. It was assumed that we would fail every week. And not just fail by actively sinning but also failing by not doing the things we should have done.

As someone who was never for a second in danger of living an unexamined life, this was unnerving. What I have done is enough fodder for constant self-examination; what I have left undone is limitless. In the years of recovery from that major depressive episode, I started to unravel these threads, to separate the migraines and depression from guilt and blame. I wasn't bad, I was sick. I wanted that knowledge to sink from my head into my gut, into the center where my true self lived, and where, I was beginning to understand, God lived, too. I came up with a plan.

Because that guilt had been so long associated with eating and weight, I started there. I decided that feeding myself was going to be my priority, above weight loss, above exercise. I was going to eat when I was hungry and not feel any shame about it. I was going to throw out all rules of dieting and simply listen to my own body's needs. I outlined two simple guidelines for myself:

1. Eat when you're hungry.
2. Stop eating when you're full.

Because I was trying to remove shame and self-recrimination from the eating process, I added a third rule:

3. Forgive yourself when you don't.

Ever since I was a child, I was stuck in a cycle of overeating, feeling shame, dieting and exercising, and then overeating again from that place of shame and hunger. I tried breaking the cycle over and over again, but I always tried to break it in the eating stage or the stopping stage. I finally realized, after years and years, that I needed to break the cycle in the shame stage. It was vital to forgive myself for eating past when I was full. From now on, I would reject shame for anything or any amount I ate.

I started out pretty well with "eat when you're hungry"—not a simple thing when you have felt your most beautiful and affirmed when you were dieting or flat-out starving yourself. I bought healthy food, prepared it, and tried to feed myself with as much love as I would feed a child and with as much purpose as I put gas in my car. But the "stop when you're full" part took a lot longer. The overeating had grown compulsive—sometimes the food just tasted so good, and I was getting such an endorphin rush from it that I couldn't stop. But other times, I was sick of eating, my jaw hurt from chewing, and the food tasted like sand, but something in me kept saying eat, eat, and I couldn't stop.

I realized that it was after a binge like that that the real opportunity for healing existed. Instead of wallowing in shame and self-hatred if I overate, I got myself a drink of water, patted myself gently on the arm and said, "That's okay. You're doing the best you can, and that's a lot! Get a good night's rest—tomorrow's another day." I even learned to thank my body for that survival instinct that kept me eating as well as being a coping mechanism that helped me through the pain of chronic illness.

As I began breaking the cycle of shame, there was a period where my overeating increased. I am grateful that I was able to go through that time because it was important in learning to trust myself and my body again. I had to reprioritize that trust in order to reconnect my body, my mind, and my spirit. I had to truly honor my own instincts over my desire to look a certain way. And, of course, there were the insidious, constant messages from culture to untangle and set aside.

But gradually, slowly, I found myself eating and thinking, "Hm, I think I'm full," and putting the food away. Without the shame, the compulsion began to diminish. Eating became a thing to enjoy and be proud of—I was giving my body what it needed to live! Exercise flowed out of that joy. Instead of beating my bad flesh into line, I was enjoying the strength in my legs as I ran and biked and in my arms as I kayaked or did yoga. Shame got me short-term success and more intense long-term problems. Forgiveness led to healing.

Ultimately what I discovered is that my stubbornness wasn't actually a flaw, much less a fatal one. It was just misdirected against myself and against others. When I learned to redirect that stubbornness toward taking care of myself and setting boundaries I needed to set, it actually opened me up to be more accepting and generous toward others. I've found that the more I'm able to forgive myself, the easier it becomes to forgive others, even those that have really hurt me.

I created a breathing exercise to both symbolize and aid that forgiveness and letting go. I breathe in, and accept everything in my past, the bad things as well as the good, grateful that they have made me who I am today. I breathe out and let go of them, freeing myself to live fully in the present moment. Then I breathe in and accept everything others have done, all the ways their lives intersected with mine, even the painful ways, and breathe it all out. And the more I let go, the less depression has to hold on to.

Breathe in: Accept.

Breathe out: Let go.

This is particularly helpful for me whenever a memory or an anxious thought triggers a physical fight-or-flight response in my body, causing me to not only relive the experiences but feel like I was unsafe in the moment. The breathing exercise helped me to address the physical aspect of this by calming and comforting my body with deep, slow breaths. It helped me internalize the spiritual aspects of forgiveness and grace by breathing those in with the oxygen that flowed through my heart and veins to my whole body. And this was a form of feeding myself as well.

Some of you may be able to relate to my issues with food and body image. But I believe the idea of feeding ourselves has a broader application than just food. Our society teaches us in a myriad of ways that our own instincts are wrong. We are encouraged to push through our natural instinct to sleep when we're tired. We are told to hold our feelings inside instead of expressing them honestly. We are told to wait our turn and pay our dues instead of allowing our uniqueness and creativity to shine.

Some of us may have been told that our romantic

and sexual desires must be controlled, limited, or denied—whether because our sexual expression falls outside the heteronormative standard or because we have been taught that sex is unacceptable outside of very specific contexts (i.e. marriage). And some of us may have been told that setting boundaries to protect ourselves emotionally, physically, and sexually is wrong even after we've been hurt repeatedly in those ways.

What would it look like to you to learn to feed yourself? Maybe, like me, it would be actual food, filling your stomach with the nutrients you need to live. Or maybe it would be letting yourself call in sick from work and rest, or gently but firmly ending a toxic relationship. Maybe it would be walking away from a community that has been harming rather than helping you. Or maybe walking toward community instead of trying to do everything on your own.

Whatever it is, learning to feed yourself is a process. You will make mistakes—don't be afraid of them. Remember that you have done the very best you can every step of the way. Breathe in. It's okay. Everything that has happened to you is part of your story. There's nothing you need to deny or forget. It has all led here, and here is where you are supposed to be right now. Breathe out—let it go. You are not defined by your pain or your mistakes or the way others have hurt you. You can let go of all of it and live fully in the moment and fully accept what this day and this moment have to offer you.

Go to sleep tonight and let the mistakes of today slip into the past. Start tomorrow fresh without needing to atone for yesterday's mistakes. Wake up, not bad, not fatally flawed, just human. Wake up, forgiven and new, and feed yourself.

Notes

1. Anne Lamott, *Traveling Mercies* (New York: Pantheon, 1999), 197–98.

16. Wanting to Die

This is a hard chapter to write. It might be a hard one to read. I'm going to talk about suicide and suicidal thoughts. If you want to skip to the next chapter, it's okay. I'll meet you there.

I've never tried to kill myself unless you count senior year in college when I starved myself every day for six months. I didn't want to die then, but life was so difficult, and I thought if I was thinner and maybe loved more, it might not be so hard. I was wrong. It was just as hard when I was thin; plus, I was anemic and undernourished. You can't live on five hundred calories a day and compliments. The end of that depression was when I started eating enough again.

I've never wanted to die, exactly, but when that last depressive episode in my thirties wore on and on, I started to lose track of my reasons to live. I thought about suicide as a concept, as one of my options, but one which I would always rule out. The medical term for this kind of thinking is suicidal ideation. My thoughts of harming myself were vague and drastic. I wrote in an earlier chapter about fantasies, and that's what the thoughts felt like. They weren't pleasant, but they weren't real. I never had a plan.

It wasn't until I found myself thinking about pills that I got scared. Pills were something I had right by my bed, a far too accessible and feasible option. I realized I had come to the point where I was considering death as an alternative to failing at work. Thankfully this realization was a wake-up call for me. As horrible as failing at my dream job would be, at least I would still be alive. I quit my job, and the relief from the pressure and stress that job created far outweighed the additional financial stress from being unemployed. The depression remained bad for a long time, but I never had suicidal ideation again. Over time, I would come to see that leaving that job wasn't failure but in fact important to my understanding that my gifts and my calling lay elsewhere.

Suicide has come close to me in other ways throughout my life. Several of my friends have talked about killing themselves and at least three have attempted it. A close family member has also been suicidal. Many of those people were struggling with more than depression: They had bipolar disorder, schizophrenia, or PTSD from childhood trauma. In some ways, a bad depressive episode can protect you from suicide by incapacitating you so much that you can't go through with it. It is actually when people are beginning to recover from a depressive episode that the risk for suicide increases.[1] It's important to keep that in mind and keep closely in touch with your therapist and doctor even if you feel like you don't need them anymore.

For me the thoughts about death were worst when I wasn't sleeping well. Insomnia often goes along with depression (as does hypersomnia—oversleeping), and for me, the first few months of that depressive episode were particularly brutal. I felt like I could maybe have made it through work difficulties, community difficulties, depression, and migraines if only I could have gotten some sleep. Eventually my doctors and I found a good combination of meds that helped me to sleep and treated the depression and migraines.

Along with the medication, I found comfort in the words of George MacDonald, a Scottish author whose children's books—*The Princess and the Goblin* and *At the Back of the North Wind*—and Victorian romance novels (heavy on theology, if you can imagine such a thing) I already loved. MacDonald believed that when we are overwhelmed and in despair, and when we feel like we want to die, it is actually more life that we are craving. He says, "When most oppressed, when most weary of life, as our unbelief would phrase it, let us bethink ourselves that it is in truth the inroad and presence of death we are weary of. When most inclined to sleep, let us rouse ourselves to live."[2]

That made sense to me. I didn't want to die—what I really wanted was to *rest* and to wake up again with renewed energy. Depression had robbed me of that natural cycle: weariness, followed by rest, followed by waking. Instead, this period of my life seemed like it was all one long night where I was always weary and inactive, but never rested. MacDonald's phrase, "the inroad and presence of death," evokes the image of an army advance, the conquering of life's rightful land by the enemy, death. What we need, MacDonald wrote, is not more death; we need more life.

He goes on to say that, "Of all things let us avoid the false refuge of a weary collapse, a hopeless yielding to things as they are. . . . He has the victory who, in the midst of pain and weakness, cries out, not for death, not for the repose of forgetfulness, but for strength to fight; for more power, more consciousness of being, more God in him."[3]

I want you to hear MacDonald's message, too, so I've changed the pronouns:

> YOU have the victory who, in the midst of pain and weakness, cry out, not for death, not for the repose of forgetfulness, but for strength to fight; for more power, more consciousness of being, more God in you.

If you feel this pull toward death—whether passively in wishing you were dead or actively in thinking about ways to die—can you identify the real need beneath it? Is it the desire to rest? Is it to relieve the pressure of work or family or other stressors? Is it because the alternative is failure or seeming failure? What would it look like for you to reach for more life instead of less? What if the thing that feels like failure, like something worse than death, is actually the way through to a much better life? That's what it ended up being for me.

Last year Bunmi Laditan wrote an achingly honest Facebook post about suicidal ideation, written as a letter to the "Enemy." In it she described how she had come close to believing the Enemy's lies. She writes,

> You . . . hit me in places that never fully healed and took advantage of my brain's weaknesses. You whispered terrible things about me to myself in my own voice until I believed them. You convinced me that it would always hurt this

much and filled me with deep shame and blinding agony.[4]

If you're in this place right now, I want you to know you're not alone. Others have fought this same battle, struggled to choose life over death, and to believe beyond hope that things would get better. I can't claim to know exactly what you're going through, or what your particular pain is. I can only offer you my own experience, my own story, and tell you that I once felt hopeless, and now there is hope. Once, tomorrow seemed like it would be just like today, and I couldn't bear that thought. But now I have come to the other side of that long night. Not that everything is better and good now, but life is life again in all its depth and beauty, pain and joy.

At the end of her letter, Bunmi rebuked the lies of the Enemy, and claimed God's love and protection over herself. Wherever you are, I pray that love and protection for you as well. You are loved and known intimately by God, your creator. Your life has value, whether you can see it or not. Keep breathing. Keep going. There are better things to come.

Notes

1. Solomon, *Noonday Demon*, 80–81.

2. George MacDonald, "Unspoken Sermons: Life," *Online Literature*, https://tinyurl.com/y4jnacv2.

3. MacDonald, "Unspoken Sermons."

4. Bunmi Laditan, "Dear Enemy," Facebook, August 5, 2018, https://tinyurl.com/y29gmmyt.

17. Loving Someone in Pain

It is out of the whirlwind that Job first hears God say "Who is this that darkens counsel by words without knowledge?" (Job 42:3). It is out of the absence of God that God makes himself present, and it is not just the whirlwind that stands for his absence, not just the storm and chaos of the world that knock into a cocked hat all man's attempts to find God in the world, but God is absent also from all Job's words about God, and from the words of his comforters, because they are words without knowledge that obscure the issue of God by trying to define him as present in ways and places where he is not present, to define him as moral order, as the best answer man can give to the problem of his life. God is not an answer man can give, God says. God himself does not give answers. He gives himself, and into the midst of the whirlwind of his absence gives himself.[1]

When she was still in her twenties, living in Spain, writer and illustrator Mari Andrew was struck out of the blue with intense pain and a paralysis that was diagnosed as Guillain-Barre syndrome, an extremely rare and aggressive autoimmune disease. She was paralyzed and in severe pain for a month, with recovery and rehab lasting much longer. Her friends tried to understand and offer support, but she found that much of what they said was unhelpful or even hurtful. In an interview with Sojourners Magazine, Mari wrote:

> It's very easy for people to say, "This will make you stronger," or even, "You're strong already, you'll get through this." But that's just not really the whole story. . . . I really appreciated people who would just tell me, "Yeah this sucks, and I can't believe you're going through this and I'm here for you and here are some flowers." That's what really helped me.[2]

One of the most difficult things for friends and family of someone with an extended illness, and maybe especially a mental illness like depression, is knowing what to say and not say. And one of the most difficult things for those going through it is having to listen to well-meant but unhelpful platitudes. A dear friend texted me a little while ago asking for advice on how to support her friends whose teenage son has been suffering from debilitating migraines for a year and a half. He is angry at God, she said, and can't believe a good God would allow this kind of suffering. His parents are afraid he is going to renounce God, and she wants to know how to be there for them.

When you are in pain and the life you know has been pulled out from under you, you naturally ask why. When you have prayed till your knees are bloody and cried out to God until your throat is hoarse, and still the pain continues, of course you wonder why a loving God is not answering you. Of course you do.

But when your friends and loved ones have prayed their own knees bloody and throats hoarse, and still you are not better, something else begins to happen. They may question God, but they may also—out loud or only in their heads—begin to question you. The blame begins to shift, slightly, to the one in pain. Are you sure you're praying enough? Are you sure you have faith that God can heal you? Are you taking the right meds? Have you tried acupuncture? Are you eating right and getting enough sleep? Have you tried everything you can?

It can be subtle or overt, but it echoes the person's own questions and doubts. Are you sure you aren't psychologically attached to the pain? Maybe you're getting something out of it. Why did you stay up late last night when you know a regular sleep schedule is shown to help depression? Maybe all of this is actually your fault? It reminds me of the questions and comments Job's friends asked him in the biblical story of Job.

Job's story has always confused me. It begins with a description of Job, a wealthy, righteous man who seeks God and spends his time and money caring for the poor. Then the scene shifts to heaven where God is bragging to Satan about Job, and Satan says that perhaps Job is only so good because God has blessed him with so much. So God gives permission for Satan to destroy all of Job's property, his animals, his servants and, horrifically, his children. When Job still perseveres and praises God, Satan asks for, and is given, permission to destroy Job's health as well, giving him painful sores all over his body as well as terrible nightmares. (From a twenty-first century perspective, I wonder how much the nightmares came from trauma and depression triggered by the loss of his children, as well as the loss of his health and prosperity.)

The rest of the book is a conversation between Job and his friends, who are all convinced that Job's suffering is because of some sin he has committed, compounded by his refusal to confess his sin and repent of it. Job alternately addresses his friends and God. At first, he begs God to let him die to end his misery, but then, he seems to shift to begging for a hearing before God to prove his innocence. His friends' words are not helping, he says; in fact, they are adding to his suffering. If I were in your place, Job says, I could make long speeches, too, but I wouldn't. I would comfort you.

In the end, God shows up "in the whirlwind" and speaks to Job of the glories of creation, telling Job that he, a mortal, can't understand God's ways. God also scolds Job's friends and tells Job to pray for them. Then God gives Job twice as much wealth as before, including new sons and daughters.

I've read the book of Job many times, and I still don't understand it. I don't understand why God would allow Job to lose his family and everything he owned. I don't understand Job's friends' advice or what God means when God shows up and silences them. And I don't understand how everything is supposed to be okay when Job gets a new family and new riches. You can't make the loss of children all better by having new children. The ending seems to ignore the grief and trauma of Job's loss and devastating illness.

I'm not the only one to have struggled with the meaning of the book of Job. Countless theologians have attempted to explain the existence of suffering and to glean the moral of the confusing story of Job. But it wasn't until I began to read the work of someone who would turn out to be another companion along the way that I found an explanation that was meaningful to me. Frederick Buechner is famous for his novels *Godric*, *The Book of Bebb*, and others, but it is his memoirs and his theological writings that have been most meaningful to me. His father died by suicide when he was ten, and Buechner speaks of profound pain and doubt from his own experience. In his book *Telling the Truth*, Buechner addresses the words of Job's friends:

> God is absent from the words of his comforters, because they are words without knowledge that obscure the issue of God by trying to define him as present in ways and places where he is not present, to define him as moral order, as the best answer man can give to the problem of his life.[3]

Our questions about pain and suffering may not have satisfying answers, or at least not answers that we can understand now. Job's friends try to explain God to him, to tell him he must not be praying enough, he must not have enough faith, or he must have some unconfessed sin or pride. And Job listens and argues with them and suffers even more because of their arguments and advice.

We try to find explanations for suffering to create a safe structure of moral order and explain bad things as the result of abandoning that moral order. It would be much easier, in some ways, if God were just a system of rules that we had to follow where good behavior was rewarded and bad behavior punished. But God is something different than that, Buechner says. "God is not an answer man can give, God says. God himself does not give answers. He gives himself, and into the midst of the whirlwind of his absence gives himself."[4]

God doesn't answer our questions, but instead gives us God's presence. And that is what we need from each other, too: Not answers, just presence—understanding, listening, acceptance, and presence. I told my friend that even if her friends' son does renounce God, the best, most loving response his parents and friends can give is not arguments, but presence. They can say to him, "It must hurt so much. I'm so sorry. I can completely understand that you would want to renounce God, and I don't love you any less for it. If God is God, God will understand, too, and not love you any less for it, either. Go ahead and cry and swear and do whatever you need to do. We're here."

I find myself thinking, too, about another character in the story, Job's wife. Everything that happened to Job has happened to her as well. Her children were killed and her home and means of support destroyed. Yet, the book centers Job and places her in the role of a scolding bystander. In fact, she suggests to Job that he should "curse God and die." In a painting by William

Blake, she gives a nasty look to the beatifically suffering Job. I think I understand, though, that her advice to Job to renounce God comes out of the pain of having just lost all that she loved. I think that a lot of our friends' and family's misplaced advice comes also from a place of pain. She is grieving, suffering poverty and scorn, and she speaks out of the bitter despair of that experience.

It occurs to me that her own despair may have been even greater than her husband's. And who was there to offer her comfort, false or otherwise? We don't really know. But we do know our own pain, and we know that others carry despair equal or greater than our own. Suffering offers us the gift of empathy, of seeing other's pain and knowing, not the specifics of their suffering, but that it must be somewhat similar to ours.

Suffering teaches us to be a gentle, comforting, nonjudgmental presence to those we love. We learn to listen. We learn not to offer advice unless advice is asked for. We learn to allow people their pain and feelings, even when those pain and feelings cause us inconvenience or anxiety. We learn, painfully, the things we wish people had offered us in the depths of our own pain, and we offer that to others. We learn to ask, "Is this what you need?" understanding that what helps us may not be what helps others.

And for those of us who are the ones struggling, we learn to let the wrong words go. We know it's not our fault that we're sick. We know damn well that we're doing the best we can to get help. We know we're strong, but that doesn't mean it's helpful to keep hearing it. When I was deep in the midst of depression and terrible migraines, a friend asked me what she could do to help me, and I found that what I really needed from her was to listen and to pray. No advice. No helpful scriptures. Just presence and lifting me up to God. And, maybe, a heartfelt, "This really sucks, Jessica. I'm so sorry."

Notes

1. Frederick Buechner, *Listening to Your Life: Daily Meditations with Frederick Buechner* (New York: Harper One, 1992), 105–6.
2. Andrew, Mari, interview with Juliet Verdal, "Mari Andrew on the 'Zigzagging Journey' of Trauma, Faith, and Art," *Sojourners*, May 2, 2018, https://tinyurl.com/yxon8s4e.
3. Buechner, *Listening to Your Life*, 105–6.
4. Buechner, *Listening to Your Life*, 105–6.

18. Finding Real-Life Community Again

> Sometimes community is made up of deep joy and deep sorrow all at once, and that is what Sabbath seems to echo. Shalom is a pronouncement of peace, of knowing that we are broken and full of grief, but that we are also beckoned into deep joy. Rest—Sabbath rest, communion rest—happens when we gather with each other and say our prayers of hope, our prayers of gratefulness, and our prayers of bare dependence on God for every good thing.
>
> ~Kaitlin Curtice[1]

Recently, Matteo and I moved into a two-bedroom apartment in an old Boston triple-decker. Our apartment is on the top floor, and due to a strange glitch in the architecture, my bedroom window looks out onto our three-season porch. Lying in my bed, I can see out the bedroom window and just past that, through the porch windows. Beyond that I see the large maple tree, one of a line of trees alongside the baseball field behind our house. When the huge and hugely bright stadium lights are lit for games, I can see the one on the other side of the field through the maple leaves. I love the layered feeling this creates—me in my bed, the rectangular window, another window beyond that, with different dimensions and shapes but all lines, parallel and perpendicular. Beyond that the rustling, moving tree branches that scoff at right angles create their own constantly shifting shapes and shadows, and beyond that, the grand, ethereal lights of the stadium are almost as bright as the sunlight but whiter and more focused, as if alien spaceships are hovering over my block.

My eyes take in the shapes and colors of this new place. I use my other senses, too—the smells and the sounds—but the visual seems to bypass the part of my brain that makes judgments and registers complaints: I dislike the meaty smell of the neighbors' early breakfast and the pounding of the bass of the cars that drive slowly down the street; I love the trumpet-filled Spanish music that the neighbors play, but sometimes it can be too loud and constant; the ice cream truck's repetition of *Turkey in the Straw* is alternately nostalgic, cheerful, and utterly annoying; I have opinions about which truck's version is better (the one that doesn't jump an octave in the middle), and I love my landlady's gentle voice as she speaks on the phone in her garden.

But the visuals come through my eyes as direct feelings—I can't say what I love, exactly, about the row of multicolored triple-deckers across the street, but I feel a jolt of happiness when I look at them. I like to move to different seats inside the apartment and observe everything—the chipped woodwork, the dark frames of the doorways, my familiar books on their familiar bookshelf, but in a new house—from different angles. I lie on the floor sometimes, to see how things look from there.

I suppose this is what painters feel, the connection to the visual that makes them want to recreate and interpret it. I'm a writer myself, so I use words to describe and make sense of things, but I'm aware that the words change the things they're describing, too. I didn't feel the words "alien" or "ethereal" when I looked out at the stadium lights last night, but I needed to use those words to describe the feeling, to move it somehow from my heart to yours, and now those words have altered it, have codified it, and the feeling will be different when I look out my window tonight. Sometimes it's worth it, to change things by describing them, to feel less alone by knowing that a few people at least will read this and feel a similar feeling reading it: Ethereal. Alien. It's necessary, really, or else I would be lost inside my own head, feeling things strongly and purely but alone. It's satisfying to gather up those feelings in a ball of dough and knead them out into something which others can taste. But I lose something, too. Safety. Surety. Purity.

****

If there's something to lose in writing, there's even more to lose in speaking. I'm so much an introvert that I think it veers into the realm of social anxiety disorder. The thing is, I love people. I love them so much. I love when they talk to me and tell me their stories. I'm just so terrified that they're going to look at me, and it's going to be my turn to speak, and I'll have nothing to say. I'm afraid that the only thing in the front of my brain will be how their bangs frame their face or how the color of their eyes is like an amber ring I once bought in Krakow and then lost in the airport bathroom, and I'll know that's not an appropriate response, but I won't be able to think of anything else.

T. S. Eliot gets at a similar feeling, I think, in his poem, "The Love Song of J. Alfred Profrock," when he writes,

> Would it have been worth while
> If one, settling a pillow or throwing off a shawl,
> And turning toward the window, should say:
> "That is not it at all,
> That is not what I meant, at all."[2]

Communicating is just so hard. Rebuilding community after trauma is hard, too. I don't go to church regularly anymore for many reasons, but the primary reason is how physically and emotionally exhausting it is. An hour and a half service plus an hour of socializing can take me out for the rest of the day. But there is a church in Boston that I think of as my church. It's called Reservoir, and the pastor is a friend of mine from college. The church recently left their denomination because of its stance against gay marriage, and their views of God, community, and service echo mine—my new views, my real views, not those I am trying to hold in order to conform.

Reservoir used to have a class called Seek for people who didn't have a gridwork for faith but were interested in learning about Christianity. They found, however, that more of the people showing up were working through bad church experiences rather than no church experiences, so they have now changed the framework of the class to helping people process those bad experiences. I met a couple who hosted a weekly gathering that had grown out of one of the original Seek classes, and they invited me to stop by. So, one night I did.

I'd only met the people there once or twice before, but as I began to talk to them, somehow, miraculously, I seemed to say things that made sense. I turned to the woman with eyes the color of amber and said—something—I'm not sure exactly what, but I meant, "Tell me your story," and she did! And when it was my turn to speak, I found I could tell a little of my story, too. And then it was like a dream, or an essay I could have written with the prompt that asks me to "Describe your perfect evening," because the husband of the woman with the amber eyes stood up and when we all fell silent, he read a spoken word poem he'd written that brought tears to all our eyes. The poem was about being separate from people and scared to come back into community and about finding the courage to step out of the safe and holy woods and come back as if from the dead. Here is a little excerpt:

> A couple years back I was part of a class here at church
> Trying to explore my faith story, a story that was in a lurch
> Because a few years before that, I had kinda lost my soul
> Became a spiritual wanderer, not knowing how to fill the hole

I looked high and low, tried reading literature to find my way
But the words didn't fill me up, and I got lonelier every day
I felt disconnected from my wife and kids, and longed to be a part
Of something bigger than myself, something with love and heart

On Sundays I'd go to the hills, seeking God as I communed with nature
And he WAS there, with me those days, but he told me I was in danger
Of isolating myself, from the great souls around me
From the people I loved, and the broader community

I tried real hard, to go it alone
But I couldn't help feeling, like a man without a home
While I looked for God in mountains, my wife explored real relationships
She and others I knew were patient, no isolating words from their lips

And over time my distrust began to melt, and I needed to be with others
Who also had questions like me, soon they'd be my sisters and brothers
I decided to explore my doubts and fears not alone but with other folk
Because going at it by myself, for me had just been a hoax

~Cully Lundgren[3]
(full poem at the end of the book)

And no one in the room said, "That is not what I meant, at all." Because it was exactly what we all meant, I think. At least it was what I meant. And we moved on from dinner to cake and Swiss chocolates, and children ran in and out of the room and knocked things over and were brushed off and forgiven. And the light in the house wasn't ethereal or alien at all, readers. I have to describe it just right because I really want you to feel what I felt. It was the light of stories being told and being listened to. It was the light of poetry. It was the light in the window when you pull up to your family's house at night after a long drive back from the city. It was the light of home.

There is a passage in C. S. Lewis' book, *Till We Have Faces*—a retelling of the Greek myth of Cupid and Psyche—in which the main character, Orual, has a revelation that the flaws she has been criticizing the gods for are in fact her own. Orual goes on to say, "I saw well why the gods do not speak to us openly, nor let us answer. Till that word can be dug out of us, why should they hear the babble that we think we mean? How can they meet us face to face till we have faces?"[4]

I've been thinking of all the times I've tried to find community and failed, and I think there were valid reasons why those groups were unhealthy or dysfunctional or just not the right fit for me. But now that I have found places in which I do feel I belong, I worry that the same thing is going to happen and that my beautiful bubble of coziness and friendship I described above is going to burst again. I was rereading *Till We Have Faces* recently, and when I got to this passage, I realized that what Orual said about the gods was true about me and my friendships. Through the crucible of depression, and in the years since that last major depressive episode, I have done so much work and experienced so much healing that I can walk into a group of people with a clearer idea of who I am. Before I was offering insecurity and confusion, but now I can offer my true face and so meet others face to face. The friendships I am building now are deeper because of it.

Of course, this becoming our true, whole selves is a process, and all groups are going to include people at various levels along the path. But I want to encourage you that as you pursue health and wholeness, not only will you begin to find the places where you best fit, you will also be able to offer them a more genuine version of yourself, and you will, in return, receive genuine friendship back. Your own work—whether it is in therapy, centering prayer, biofeedback, working through the Enneagram, using cognitive behavioral techniques, or something entirely different that you have found to help you learn and grow—will strengthen your community as well as yourself. You may even find that you begin to create community yourself, drawing people around the cozy fire of your own spirit.

Notes

1. Kaitlin B. Curtice, *Glory Happening* (Brewster, MA: Paraclete, 2017), 24.
2. Eliot, *Prufrock and Other Observations*, 9–16.
3. Cully Lundgren, 2017, unpublished. Used with permission.
4. C. S. Lewis, *Till We Have Faces* (New York: Harvest, 1956), 294.

Epilogue: What You Have Gained, You Have Gained

> When suddenly you seem to lose all you thought you gained, do not despair. Your healing is not a straight line. You must accept setbacks & regressions. Don't say, "All is lost, I have to start all over again." This isn't true. What you have gained you have gained.
> ~Henri Nouwen[1]

> His glory might not bring the dead back to life, but his glory that is made perfect in my brokenness could bring the dead within others back to life. Will there still be questions without answers? Yes. But I don't think answers are what we are looking for anyway. I think we're looking for grace, enough that we can manage the pain with. And answers are not grace; they're just information. Empathy is grace. Company is grace. "Me too." That's grace.
> ~Matt Bays[2]

I've been reading *Sabbatical Journey* by Henri Nouwen, his journal from the last year of his life. Of course Henri didn't know it was his last year of life as he is writing, and many of his thoughts are for his future plans. He was only sixty-five, my parents' age. It's hard sometimes to read his thoughts about the future, his plans for ministry and writing. The journal goes through August 1996, and he died of a heart attack in September that same year.

At the time Nouwen is writing *Sabbatical Journey*, it had been eight years since the period of intense depression and spiritual struggle which he wrote about in *The Inner Voice of Love*. As I write this book, it has also been about eight years since my friend, Matteo, gave me *The Inner Voice of Love*, a time when I was going through my own period of depression and struggle, and Nouwen's words helped carry me through my own anguished journey. It feels significant to me to be reading *Sabbatical Journey* (also given to me by Matteo) eight years after *The Inner Voice of Love*, just as Nouwen wrote the books eight years apart.

In the *Sabbatical Journey*, Nouwen talks about opening up to a friend concerning his ongoing struggles:

> In the early evening Nathan and I had a nice dinner. At one point we talked about the anxiety that had been plaguing me during the last few months. I felt somewhat embarrassed and ashamed to put my inner burden on my best friend, but, in the end, I am glad I did. Nathan told me that he found it hard, not so much to listen to my pain, but to realize that I had walked with it so long without sharing it. I explained that it had not been possible for me to talk

about such things on the telephone, and he understood. That was a comfort for me. I sometimes wonder how I am going to survive emotionally.[3]

I read this, curled up on my quiet couch on a winter evening, hands wrapped around a hot cup of tea. Nouwen's time of depression, eight years prior to writing about Nathan, lasted for about six months. My own, eight years ago, lasted longer—two years, perhaps, with another three or four before I was well out of it and another year or two before I left the community that had been such a mix of security and trauma, comfort and conflict.

Nouwen wrote his journal with the intention of publishing it. He was going to do the editing himself, but after he died his friend Susan took on the task. After I read that paragraph last night, I set down the book and picked up my own journal. I feel I share so much with Nouwen—the inner struggle, the experience living in community, good friends to walk through my life with me, and the desire and calling to write down my experience to give to others. Nouwen wrote around forty books in his life, books full of such wisdom and healing, such intimacy with God and striving to live a life of love and service. His writing helped me and so many others move through anguish to freedom. Yet even at the end, two months before his death, he wrote that stark, honest sentence: "I sometimes wonder how I am going to survive emotionally."

I imagine him, like me, curled up on his own couch, journal in hand. He had so much insight, so much wisdom to give to us. But in the end, his greatest gift was his honesty and vulnerability. We all desire healing and strength, but when the apostle Paul begged God for his own thorn in the flesh to be taken away, God did not heal him, but instead said to him, "My grace is sufficient for you, for my power is made perfect in weakness."[4] I don't understand exactly why or how, but God values us in our weakness as much as in our strength. So here is my weakness, my illness, my struggle. It is my gift to you because it is what I was given to offer.

Thank you for reading this book. It might seem strange, but I've felt your presence here with me as I write. I hope I'm not just writing a book. I hope I am creating a space for you and I to sit with each other, to listen to each other. Here, let us be willing to be weak in front of each other. Let us teach each other out of what we do not know as well as what we do. Let us learn to value each other's weakness as well as strength. Let us say to each other that we find it hard, not to listen to each other's pain, but to realize that we had walked with it so long without sharing it.

Love,
Jessica

Notes

1. Nouwen, *Inner Voice of Love*, 38.

2. Matt Bays, *Finding God in the Ruins: How God Redeems Pain* (Colorado Springs: David C. Cook, 2016), 124.

3. Henri Nouwen, *Sabbatical Journey: The Diary of His Final Year* (New York: Crossroad, 1998), 207.

4. 2 Cor 5:9.

Acknowledgments

I am so grateful for the people who have supported me, both through the process of writing and through the process of learning about my own depression and recovering from it.

For my amazing and patient editor Lisa Kloskin and for Fortress Press for believing in me.

For Olga Grlic for her incredible cover art.

For Crystal Cheatham, Sandi Villarreal, and Josh Larson for publishing my work.

For my parents, Matthew and Christine, and my aunts Deb and Diane for their constant support and encouragement.

For my brother David for his steady affection and for offering his home as an option in crises and providing cats to snuggle.

For Gina for being my phone-a-friend for twenty-seven years now.

For my writing community who offered insight, guidance, and compassion, and offered to fight the bad guys for me—Arwen, Judith, Omar, Judi, Matt, Susan, Tyler, Shannon, Callie, James, Layton, Rachel, Kaitlin, Fen, Ivy, Aimee, Lisa, Cis, Anna, Kate, Jessa, Sarah, Charlotte, Karen, Jason, Beth, Nicole, Tracie, and so many more.

For Laura and Glennon who have been my own personal cheering squad for five years and I don't know how I got so lucky.

For Mark, Kelly, Mallory, and Cameron, for being my home away from home, wherever you go.

For Daniela, Joel, Shannon, and all at GH for fighting alongside me for community, even when the battle drew our own blood.

For Scott and Ivy for setting a table for the most beautiful collection of faithful doubters I've ever met, and for Steve and all those who set the broader table at Reservoir.

For Glennon, Abby, Amanda, Liz, Katherine, Gloria, and all at Together Rising for letting me be a part of helping others even when I could barely take care of myself.

For Miriam, Sarah, and Claudia who always make me feel like a celebrity when I walk in the door, and for Allison for her steady, generous friendship.

For Eleanor and Samuel for their excitement for me, especially when Paperback Writer comes on, and for helping me pick out my author photo. We are in a book!

For Carrie and Megan for permission for the dedication. I miss them, too.

For so many friends who read and share my writing with such enthusiasm, it would be impossible to name you all without leaving someone out, so just THANK YOU.

And, of course, for Matteo, who doesn't need effusive expressions of affection but for whom, nevertheless, this whole book is one long thank you letter.

Appendix: Further Resources

FOR MENTAL HEALTH CRISES

The National Suicide Prevention Lifeline offers "24/7, free and confidential support for people in distress, prevention and crisis resources for you or your loved ones, and best practices for professionals." You can call them at 1-800-273-8255 or go to their website to chat. https://suicidepreventionlifeline.org/

The National Alliance on Mental Illness offers many resources, including a crisis text line (text NAMI to 741-741) and information about local support groups. Their website also has numbers to call for domestic abuse (800-799-7233) and sexual abuse (800-656-4673) crises. https://www.nami.org/

The Youth Mental Health Project "is a grassroots organization whose primary purpose is to educate, empower, and support families and communities so they will have knowledge, skills, and resources they need to support the social, emotional, mental, and behavioral health of youth." http://ymhproject.org/

BOOKS

The following are books that I either quote in this book, or read for research, or just really love and want to recommend.

Books about depression and mental illness:

Andrew Solomon, *The Noonday Demon: An Atlas of Depression*
This is an excellent and very thorough atlas of depression's history, symptoms, treatment, and much more, told with stories of the author's own struggles as well as those of others.

Gerald May, *The Dark Night of the Soul: A Psychiatrist Explores the Connection Between Darkness and Spiritual Growth*

Clement Hawk: *CBT For Depression: An Unconventional Guide to Overcome Depression, Eliminate Negative Thoughts, and Feel Better*

Memoirs about depression and other mental illness:

Henri Nouwen, *The Inner Voice of Love: A Journey Through Anguish to Freedom* and *Sabbatical Journey: The Diary of His Final Year*
(Nouwen doesn't specifically say that he was clinically depressed, but so much of what he wrote resonates with my own experience of depression.)

Meri Nana-Ama Danquah, *Willow Weep for Me: A Black Woman's Journey Through Depression*

Terese Marie Mailhot, *Heart Berries: A Memoir*

Alia Joy: *Glorious Weakness: Discovering God in All We Lack*

Books about trauma:

Bessel Van Der Kolk, *The Body Keeps the Score: Brain, Mind, and Body in the Healing of Trauma*

Books about surviving childhood sexual assault:

Laura Parrott Perry, *She Wrote it Down: How a Secret-Keeper Became a Storyteller*

Matt Bays, *Finding God in the Ruins: How God Redeems Pain*

Books about contemplative and centering prayer:

Ed Cyzewski, *Flee, Be Silent, Pray: An Anxious Evangelical Finds Peace with God Through Contemplative Prayer*

Jeanne Guyon, *Experiencing the Depths of Jesus Christ*

Thomas Keating, *Open Mind, Open Heart: The Contemplative Dimension of the Gospel* and *Invitation to Love: The Way of Christian Contemplation*

Basil Pennington, *Centering Prayer: Renewing an Ancient Christian Prayer Form*

Thomas Merton, *New Seeds of Contemplation*

Other books by Christian mystics:

Teresa of Avila, *Interior Castle*

Therese of Lisieux, *The Autobiography of St. Therese of Lisieux*

St. John of the Cross, *Dark Night of the Soul*

Anonymous, *The Cloud of Unknowing*

Books about faith-shifts:

Sarah Bessey, *Out of Sorts: Making Peace with an Evolving Faith* and *Jesus Feminist: An Invitation to Revisit The Bible's View of Women*

Barbara Brown Taylor, *Learning to Walk in the Dark* and *Leaving Church: A Memoir of Faith*

Rachel Held Evans, *Searching for Sunday: Loving, Leaving, and Finding the Church* and *Inspired: Slaying Giants, Walking on Water, and Loving the Bible Again* and *Faith Unraveled: How a Girl Who Had All The Answers Learned to Ask Questions*

Books about community:

Dietrich Bonhoeffer, *Life Together: The Classic Exploration of Faith in Community*

Deidra Riggs, *One: Unity in a Divided World*

Layton Williams, *Holy Disunity: How What Separates Us Can Save Us*

Books about chronic illness:

Kate Bowler, *Everything Happens for a Reason: And Other Lies I've Loved*

Tanya Marlow, *Those Who Wait: Finding God in Disappointment, Doubt and Delay*

Books about the Enneagram:

Don Richard Riso and Russ Hudson, *The Wisdom of the Enneagram: The Complete Guide to Psychological and Spiritual Growth for the Nine Personality Types*

Ian Morgan Cron and Suzanne Stabile, *The Road Back to You: An Enneagram Journey to Self-Discovery*

Richard Rohr, *The Enneagram: A Christian Perspective*

Hannah Paasch, *Millenneagram: The Enneagram Guide for Discovering Your Truest, Baddest Self*

Books by some more of my favorite companions on the road:

Madeleine L'Engle, *A Circle of Quiet: The Crosswicks Journal, Book 1*

Glennon Doyle, *Carry on Warrior: Thoughts on Life Unarmed* and *Love Warrior: A Memoir*

Jomny Sun, *Everyone's a Aliebn When Ur a Aliebn Too: A Book*

Lin-Manuel Miranda and Jonny Sun, *Gmorning, Gnight!: Little Pep Talks for Me & You*

Mari Andrew, *Am I There Yet?: The Loop-de-loop, Zigzagging Journey to Adulthood*

Frederick Buechner, *Wishful Thinking: A Seeker's ABC* and *Whistling in the Dark: A Doubter's Dictionary*

Kaitlin Curtice, *Glory Happening: Finding the Divine in Everyday Places*

Emmy Kegler, *One Coin Found: How God's Love Stretches to the Margins*

Poetry:

Poetry has a way of bypassing our rational mind and getting to the heart of our feelings and experiences. Below are a few of my favorite books of poetry, some of which I quote in this book, and some which I just really love.

Tanaya Winder: *Why Storms Are Named After People and Bullets Remain Nameless*

Bunmi Laditan, *Dear Mother: Poems on the Hot Mess of Motherhood*

Rainer Maria Rilke, *The Book of Hours*

Mary Szybist, *Incarnadine*

Jennifer Michael Hecht, *Who Said*

T.S. Eliot, *The Love Song of J. Alfred Prufrock* and *Four Quartets*

Mary Oliver, *Dream Work* and *Blue Horses*

WEBSITES

Ekhartyoga.com
This is my favorite website for doing yoga at home. Esther Ekhart has taught me so much, both about

yoga and mindfulness, and there are several other teachers as well and hundreds of classes that you can search by teacher, length, and type. As of this printing they offer two weeks free to new members, so you can try them out.

qchristian.org
According to their website, Q Christian Fellowship "cultivates radical belonging among LGBTQ+ people and allies through a commitment to growth, community, and relational justice."

adaa.org/diverse-communities
The Anxiety and Depression Association of America recognizes that minority groups have specific risks and treatment needs, and lists resources for African Americans, Latinx, Asian-Americans, LGBTQ+ individuals, and those with low income.

This is the full poem I quote in chapter 18. Cully wrote it as an introduction to the Seek class offered at Reservoir Church in Cambridge, Massachusetts, a safe place for people to process difficult or traumatic experiences with church and religion.

SEEK TO ME
by Cully Lundgren

A couple years back I was part of a class here at church

Trying to explore my faith story, a story that was in a lurch

Because a few years before that, I had kinda lost my soul

Became a spiritual wanderer, not knowing how to fill the hole

I looked high and low, tried reading literature to find my way

But the words didn't fill me up, and I got lonelier every day

I felt disconnected from my wife and kids, and longed to be a part

Of something bigger than myself, something with love and heart

On Sundays I'd go to the hills, seeking God as I communed with nature

And he WAS there, with me those days, but he told me I was in danger

Of isolating myself, from the great souls around me

From the people I loved, and the broader community

I tried real hard to go it alone

But I couldn't help feeling like a man without a home

While I looked for God in mountains, my wife explored real relationships

She and others I knew were patient, no isolating words from their lips

And over time my distrust began to melt, and I needed to be with others

Who also had questions like me, soon they'd be my sisters and brothers

I decided to explore my doubts and fears not alone but with other folk

Because going at it by myself, for me had just been a hoax

On Sundays I started coming to church, it felt good to be with family and friends

And I stopped detaching from those I knew, but I kept asking questions

Lo and behold, I came to find many others were on a similar journey

With doubts, fears and dubiousness, about God, religion, and meaning

So some time later I entered into a class here called SEEK

Been happening here a while, a safe place for questioners to meet

Others like them who aren't so sure, about what it means to follow Jesus

At SEEK they can ask any question, it's a way to put together some of those pieces

Of life and experience that have made us each who we are

And to inquire with other seekers, whether their views are similar or apart

The class brings together people from all over this great town

Allowing you to have difficult conversations, to lay your questions down

SEEK is lacking in judgement, of the story you bring to the table

Just come with your questions, this group's real, it's not a fable